T0198657

THE GIFT OF A LIFETIME

Building a Marriage That Lasts

Revised Edition

Barbara J. Peters, RN, LPC

authorHOUSE®

AuthorHouse™
1663 Liberty Drive
Bloomington, IN 47403
www.authorhouse.com
Phone: 1 (800) 839-8640

Published by AuthorHouse 09/19/2019

ISBN: 978-1-4490-4658-3 (sc)
ISBN: 978-1-4490-4659-0 (hc)
ISBN: 978-1-4490-4657-6 (e)

Print information available on the last page.

Front cover picture by Capucine Henry Photographe.

Scripture taken from the Holy Bible, New International Version®. Copyright © 1973, 1978, 1984 Biblica. Used by permission of Zondervan. All rights reserved.

This book is printed on acid-free paper.

Because of the dynamic nature of the Internet, any web addresses or links contained in this book may have changed since publication and may no longer be valid. Case studies are fabricated to show common relationship problems seen in counseling, or are changed to protect the confidentiality of clients; any resemblance to actual persons, living or dead, or actual events is purely coincidental. This book is not intended as a substitute for a reader needing medical or psychological advice specific to a unique problem. The reader is encouraged to consult a counseling professional in matters relating to physical and mental health. The views expressed in this work are solely those of the author and do not necessarily reflect the views of the publisher, and the publisher hereby disclaims any responsibility for them.

Presented to:

_____

By:

_____

On the Occasion of:

_____

Date:

_____

Dedication

I lovingly dedicate this book to my grandchildren: Briana, Lexa, Katherine, and Dylan.

I hope that one day each of you will be blessed with a marriage that lasts for a lifetime.

Contents

Acknowledgments

A special thank you . . .

To Larry James, for his encouragement and inspiring foreword.

To my clients, who trust me to help them with their relationships.

To Sara Hines Martin, a fellow therapist and writer, for her encouragement and assistance.

To Bob Frederick, my good friend and colleague, for his input and expertise on alcohol and drug use.

To the many professionals who have influenced my concepts on marriage, especially to John Gray and Dr. Jim McCormick.

To Virginia Davis, for editing the book.

Foreword

As you read this book, I would like for you to ask yourself a number of questions:

Am I someone I'd like to be in a relationship with?
Who would I have to become to have a great relationship?
What could I do differently?
Whose assistance could I request?
How would I change? Or would I?
Am I willing to stop trying to change my partner?

Miracles occur in relationships when two people who really love each other work together and stay focused on the solutions that build a strong relationship, rather than get wrapped up in the problems that may be dragging it down.

Barbara Peters skillfully presents a treasure trove of tips, suggestions, and case studies that will help you find answers.

I perform more than seventy-five romantic weddings each year. As a wedding minister, I have coached hundreds of couples about relationships as I interviewed them prior to their wedding ceremony. In their rush to be married, many of them did not have a clue about what to expect after their wedding.

Here are several tips that I always pass along to my wedding clients. The tips all support Barbara's gift of a lifetime. In my experience, there are two most common problems that occur in relationships.

First is about communications. It's important to communicate with love. Here is an interesting way to think about this. Sometimes communication is more about what we don't say but should. I call this "undelivered communications." It is those things we know we should talk about but don't. Be in constant communication about what you want and need, and what you don't want.

Trust is the very foundation of a healthy love relationship. There can be no trust without conversation, no genuine intimacy without trust. One of the secrets to having a healthy love relationship is to never be afraid to openly and honestly discuss whatever is relevant to the success of the relationship.

The second most common problem in relationships is unfulfilled expectations. A problem occurs when we expect our partner to love us a certain way, and when he or she does not, we are disappointed. Disappointment often leads to resentment, frustration, anger and worse. In other words, we must always love our partners for who they are, not for who we think they should be.

Remember, relationships are something that must be worked on all the time, not only when they are broken and need to be fixed. Never stop doing the things that brought you together in the first place. Surprise your partner with romantic moments from the past.

I am glad that some therapists around the country share my desire that couples can have lifelong marriages. Barbara Peters is one of those therapists who has committed her talents to helping couples achieve that dream.

Celebrate Love!

Larry James
Scottsdale, Arizona

P.S. Remember to say, "I love you," (out loud) at least once every day!

Larry James is a non-denominational minister, professional speaker, relationship coach and author of three relationship books: How to Really Love the One You're With; LoveNotes for Lovers: Words that Make Music for Two Hearts Dancing; and Red Hot LoveNotes for Lovers.
He has won awards for his "romantic" wedding ceremony. He is President of CelebrateLove.com and CelebrateIntimateWeddings.com.

A Personal Note from the Author

A friend of mine lost his wife of many years due to a long-term illness. He had The Gift of which I am writing. During his wife's final days, he stayed by her.

Later he told me, "I'll never forget the wonderful experiences we had together."

He showed that a satisfying lifetime marriage is attainable, that life is uncertain, and that we shouldn't waste time being unhappy. Instead, let's work to build lifetime marriages.

A Personal Note from the Author

The most common wedding vow in America

Groom: I, (Name), take you, (Name), to be my wife, to have and to hold, from this day forward, for better or for worse, for richer, for poorer, in sickness and in health, to love and to cherish, 'til death do us part. And hereto I pledge you my faithfulness.

Bride: I, (Name), take you, (Name), to be my husband, to have and to hold, from this day forward, for better or for worse, for richer, for poorer, in sickness and in health, to love and to cherish, 'til death do us part. And hereto I pledge you my faithfulness.

Introduction

So, you have said, "I do" and promised to love and to cherish until death do you part. You have just made one of the most important decisions of your life, and now you feel as if you are beginning your journey, riding off into the sunset to live happily ever after. What could go wrong?

In some wedding services, a wedding officiate may say, "Marriage is not a state in which to enter into lightly." Some individuals, however, give little thought before entering into that holy state. They leap into it with the expectation that the other partner will make them happy. If the officiating person were to ask, "Are you willing to work every day for the rest of your life to make this marriage a satisfying union?" Do you think that would make a difference in marriages?

Many individuals do not realize that marriage requires more than a commitment; it requires constant work and maintenance every day to be successful. Just as we have promised to love, honor, and cherish, we must care for our marriage and feed it every day just as we do our bodies.

I am pleased you have chosen this book; I believe it will help preserve your marriage vows. I firmly believe in the institution of marriage. Since marriage is the most meaningful of all human relationships, I want to see it live on.

The marriage contract is a sacred covenant and should be treated with respect and honor between the two people who marry. In our rapidly changing society, with so many things out of our control, we need to focus on family and on what we can do to keep families together. From the beginning, marriage takes work and daily maintenance in order to succeed. The work is mostly on yourself as you try to be the very best person you can be for your spouse. It is not about finding the right person, but about being the right person. By becoming the type of person you would like to spend a lifetime with, you can give that gift to your spouse.

The unique approach that I bring to couples, both in my practice and in this book, involves understanding that marriage depends on the FACTS, an acronym which stands for forgiveness, acceptance, compassion, trust and spirituality. These are qualities that a strong married couple demonstrates to each other in their loving relationship. The qualities represented by the FACTS are further extended by another acronym, FAITH.

FAITH stands for friendship, affection, intimacy, time, and happiness, and these are the gifts you bring to yourself and your spouse by practicing a healthy marriage. For a clear understanding, think of FACTS as habits or practices and FAITH as the fruit those actions cultivate that spouses must seek. You wouldn't plant seeds for an apple orchard and then not show up to get the harvest at the end, would you?

I want to present you this book as a gift, because your marriage is a lifetime gift that you and your spouse present to each other. I want to help couples enjoy a lifetime of satisfaction without experiencing the trauma of divorce.

When a couple finds themselves out of marital bliss and teetering on divorce, they often enter the counseling process. It is here that they discover that fulfillment in marriage does not come automatically after saying "I do" but requires work to achieve lasting happiness. It is to this endeavor that I have chosen to dedicate myself to couples counseling.

Writing this book has been a labor of love; it is my hope that by reading this book, you will find the answers to help you keep your marriage healthy. After you do this, you may not only lovingly bestow this gift to yourself, but to others.

"Miracles can happen if you work hard and are consistent."

~ Barbara J. Peters

Chapter One

Why I Believe I Can Bestow this Gift

Marital problems became a reality to me at the early age of four when my parents separated for eight years. My brother, ten years my senior, acted in a parental role. When my parents reunited, I was a teenager experiencing all the hormonal changes of teenage life; I was more interested in my peers - and their acceptance of me - than in bonding with my father, who had just rejoined our family.

Since I already had issues with my father that would eventually affect my own relationships, I had difficulty accepting his reentry into the family. The transition was made more difficult when my brother got married and moved out at the same time my father moved in. It was no surprise that I had problems in my first romantic relationship, which later caused me to seek counseling. That counseling experience was beneficial because I learned some of the elements that comprise a healthy relationship.

Later, when I pursued counseling as a career, I grew in my understanding of the complexities of relationships. To become a counselor, it helps to receive counseling as part of your education. Through much study and professional experience, I have learned what is needed to have a lasting relationship. Much of my knowledge came from the clients in my private practice as a counselor. From their stories and the work we did together, I was able to see the cause and effect of their disillusionment with marriage. I knew that I needed to find a way to share this knowledge and experience with others. In retrospect, I wish someone could have given me this gift when I was twenty-one years old and ready to take that important step of saying "I do." But I know that without those experiences (both good and bad), I would not be able to give you this gift today.

I remember a professor saying, while I was getting my counseling degree, "You are never an expert because there is always another question to ask." Since then, asking questions has enriched my life and my practice and has become one of my favorite pastimes. I have often heard clients tell me that my questions made them see things differently. Their responses often yielded more information and insight into their unique situations.

When I began my practice, I knew that I had a strong interest in couples counseling. I took continuing education courses and started researching the experts in the field. Before long, I developed a passion and felt energized by the work, especially when couples expressed satisfaction in their marriages based on their counseling experience. It became a labor of love, and as my five year-old granddaughter says, "I do work in kindergarten, but it doesn't feel like work because I have fun." I, too, call what I do work, but many times it feels like fun instead, especially when I see a sparkle in clients' eyes, and they report they no longer need my services.

Throughout my practice, I have counseled mostly heterosexual married couples. Other relationships carry many of the same dynamics, and any committed relationship can benefit from professional therapy. However, because my current client base consists of heterosexual couples, this group has provided the background and experience for my book.

From reading this book you will discover what it takes to make your marriage a loving and lasting one, how to make each moment count, and how to create your own miracle. While I do not perform magic, I do give you the tools to be your own magician and make miracles happen. With my knowledge, ideas, and experience as a counselor and in my own life, I give you the opportunity to have a relationship that can last a lifetime.

> "

"Marriage, at its best, is one of God's greatest gifts. Marriage is intended to be the deepest and most meaningful of all human relationships; and, it can be, if rightly understood and lovingly approached. But, it is not easy and does not come naturally. Marriage must be understood realistically and worked at diligently; otherwise, that which is intended to be so good can become miserable."

~ Dr. James R. McCormick

Chapter Two

Reasons for Saving Your Marriage

This chapter is addressed to couples who are married but struggling with some aspect of their relationship. Once upon a time, you said, "I do" and made a lifelong commitment to another person. What was the setting of your wedding? It may have only been you, your spouse, and a marriage officiate, but still, you made a promise. Do you remember why you made that commitment?

Try not to think about the past few months or years that may bring memories of difficulties, but remember your courtship and the early days of your marriage. Recall the reasons you chose each other, the common interests you had and the love you felt. That was before you possibly started taking your spouse for granted or started focusing on the things you would like to change about your spouse. A person must want to change and make those changes themselves.

People get married for many reasons – for legal, social or economic security; others marry in order to have children and raise a family; and some people often marry to obtain citizenship or the legal right to remain in the country. The best reason is that a couple is in love and wants to spend the rest of their lives together.

Legal sources define marriage as a contractual relationship giving equal rights to both people, acknowledged by the state, a religious authority, or both, in which it is consummated. Socially and emotionally, people view marriage as a permanent commitment between two lovers for a lifetime. How individuals define their own marriage is indeed open for interpretation, and the way two people define their own marriage often paves the way they live together as a couple.

Dr. James R. McCormick, in his book, *Marriage Is for Adults*, gives a wonderful example of commitment: "I am convinced that there is no depth relationship without pain, and those people who cut and run when the going gets tough, never stay together long enough to get the

5

real joy of the relationship." He continues with, "It is only through commitment to be together from now on out, no matter what, that a couple stays together long enough to get to the genuine joys of marriage..... Depth and authentic joy come only through the sharing of difficulty together."

Research has shown that individuals who are happily married live longer and healthier lives than either divorced people or unhappily married ones. According to a study by Stack and Eshleman titled "Marital Status and Happiness: A 17-Nation Study" (1998), marriage positively impacts an individual's life. They conclude "married persons have a significantly higher level of happiness than persons who are not married. This effect was independent of financial and health-oriented protections offered by marriage."

Research has also proven that marriage has a greater impact on our lives than most people understand. Researcher Maggie Gallager explains, "Men and women who remain in their first marriage enjoy significantly higher levels of physical and mental health. People who are married have higher incomes and enjoy greater emotional support" (Waite and Gallagher, 2000). This is true not only in America but in seventeen other countries, according to Gallager's research: "Unmarried people spend twice as much time as patients in hospitals as their married peers and have lower activity levels." Dr. Linda Waite conducted a study which revealed that "86% of unhappily married people who stick it out, find that, five years later, their marriages are happier. Three-fifths who said their marriages were unhappy in the late 1980's and who stayed married, said their marriages were either very happy or happy when interviewed in the early 1990's."

Dr. Robert Coombs, Professor of Biobehavioral Sciences at the UCLA School of Medicine, in his review of more than 130 empirical studies on how marriage impacts well being, found that seventy percent of chronic problem drinkers were divorced or separated, and that single men are three times more likely to die of cirrhosis of the liver than married men. The highest rates of mental disorders are found among the single and divorced.

Although many young women have a fairy tale notion about marriage, thinking their husband will be the answer to all their needs, marriage is not a romantic fantasy. It is, instead, a psychological journey that begins with attraction, travels through a course of self-discovery, and culminates in a satisfying lifelong union. It is forever changing as we are in constant growth while we travel life's fluid path. It is not about finding the perfect mate, but working on yourself to become the perfect mate for the spouse you have chosen.

If you are in an unhappy marriage and have been contemplating divorce, this book may be just what you need to reassure you that there is a way to make your commitment work. The fact that you have started reading this book is an indication that you really want things to work between you and your partner. Developing an action plan to save your marriage from this fate is the antidote. Hopefully, putting the FACTS into practice and appreciating the fruits of FAITH - as I explain beginning in Chapter Four - will help you to concentrate on doing the beautiful work of saving your marriage.

Some Extra Thought: Divorces in the U.S.

According to statistics compiled in 2005 by the U.S. Census Bureau, there were approximately 2,230,000 marriages in 2005, down from approximately 2,279,000 the previous year. The divorce rate that year was 3.6 (per 1,000) people - the lowest rate since 1970. Nevada had the highest divorce rate (because divorce is fast and simple there and people come from other states for a quick divorce) and the District of Columbia had the lowest.

New figures compiled in 2008 show the divorce rate seemed to be declining slightly. Three reasons for this are:

1. Fewer marriages are taking place. Now, more people are choosing to live together without a legal commitment.
2. Many people are entering into prenuptial agreements, making people think about the serious step they are making before taking the marriage leap.
3. More people are entering into counseling to save their marriages. Some couples are even seeking premarital counseling, because the prevention of an unhappy marriage can save a couple from a lot of heartache. Today, many work places are offering counseling as part of their insurance packages or employee benefits. Employers realize that people who are happy at home will perform better in the work place.

John Gottman, one of the country's foremost relationship experts, claims he can predict whether a couple will stay together or end in divorce after listening to the couple interact in his "Love Lab" for as little as five minutes. He goes on to report in his book *The Seven Principles for Making Marriages Work* that marriages do not fail because of arguments, but because of how arguments take place. Gottman's findings are relevant because he has done his homework. In his "Love Lab" he has studied more than seven hundred couples and followed them over time to make his predictions. His book, along with a library of exercises and interventions, has become an important part of my practice.

"Solution-focused therapy respects clients' own resources and is directed toward building solutions rather than increasing insight into putative maladaptive psychological mechanisms. It is optimistic, collaborative, future-oriented, user-friendly, and often effective."

~ Clinical Handbook of Couple Therapy

Chapter Three

How Do You Know if You Need Counseling?

What does couples counseling try to do for a couple? How do you know if your relationship needs it? If you are engaged and haven't yet made the big commitment, premarital counseling is a good idea, and a way to eliminate some unpleasant surprises. If you are married and experiencing challenges in relating to your spouse, the earlier you involve yourself in some kind of couples counseling, the sooner you can identify the issues in your relationship.

Premarital counseling

Everyone remembers Forrest Gump saying, "Life is like a box of chocolates. You never know what you are going to get." Yes, life is like a box of chocolates, but in choosing a partner for life, it is very important to know exactly what you are going to get.

When two people meet, they bring a vast collection of differences to their relationship. There may be religious differences, educational differences, geographic differences, cultural differences, financial differences, and possibly children from a previous marriage. All these factors can produce difficulties. These issues should be discussed prior to the marriage, and the couple should arrive at an understanding of how these factors will affect the marriage. This is where pre-marital counseling can help.

While pre-marital counseling does not guarantee that the couple will have a successful marriage, it often prevents an unhappy marriage from taking place. It is like an insurance policy and can serve to prevent the disappointments that may be felt with the passage of time. It offers an opportunity to explore differences, hopes, and dreams in a safe and supportive environment. Sometimes the effect will be to postpone the marriage until the differences are resolved. In general, most couples find some benefit in knowing the challenges they will face.

There are several types of pre-marital counseling. Sometimes the clergyman or woman who will be performing the ceremony provides this service, as well as private counselors. The goal is to address the obstacles and threats to marital happiness, and help prepare couples for their future together. My model for this - solution-focused therapy - involves an initial assessment of individual goals and personalities while identifying some family-of-origin factors. It also involves some training in communication skills, and finally, a development of a long-term plan of action to help keep love alive.

Marital counseling

If you are married and think that your marriage is in trouble, consider the following: all couples have disagreements. When the disagreements become regular, and when they seem to produce poor solutions, these are warning signs. When couples stop talking about things because they cannot agree or because they have problems coming to compromise, it is a sign of disengagement. When couples start leading parallel lives without interaction or connection to each other, a red flag is starting to wave. When there is no more fun, just daily tasks, and going through the motions of an everyday life, then something is seriously wrong. When the relationship changes drastically from what it was in the beginning, this is a warning sign. When someone feels lonely within the relationship, she or he needs to stop and look at what is happening.

No one is perfect, and therefore no relationship will be perfect. When couples begin to find themselves in troubled waters, counseling might help them get back on track. But, if you do decide to find a counselor, how would you go about it?

Often a friend, doctor, or insurance company can recommend a counselor. Maybe you peruse the Internet or the listings in the telephone directory. Whatever your method, it is a good idea to arrive at the first session with an open mind. It is important that you feel comfortable and relaxed with the counselor.

Your counselor is not there to judge or intimidate you, but to help you. What is said to the counselor will be kept in confidentiality. It is important that both parties feel they can be honest with and trust the counselor to help with their relationship. They must also realize that it will take more than one session - or even several - to resolve their problems. They must be willing to follow the recommendations of the counselor and do their homework. If, after the first session, the couple believes the counselor cannot be helpful, they should not give up on counseling, but find another counselor. Sometimes one must visit two or three counselors before finding the perfect fit.

Tips to make counseling work for you

- Couples should come in quickly before the problem has become severe and before both husband and wife have detached to such an extent that reattachment is difficult. Many couples wait several years after problems start to seek help. Each person has a lot of scar tissue by then. Often they no longer have any friendship left, but have become adversaries. When someone has a physical injury, there is a window of time for getting medical help/medication/therapy, etc. before the situation becomes solidified and resistant to treatment. A similar dynamic applies in human relationships; the sooner the parties take action when conflict takes place or distance occurs, the sooner the situation can be turned around.

- Have realistic expectations about what a therapist can accomplish. Many people expect the professional to wave a magic wand and make all the problems disappear.

- Don't expect the marriage to be turned around in a few sessions. Take a look at how long the marriage has been in trouble; that will indicate the length of time it will take to turn things around. (That does not mean that the time will match exactly.) Turning a marriage around could be compared to turning around a gigantic ocean liner; it takes time.

- Don't expect that simply attending sessions will rescue the marriage. While the activities that take place in the office can make significant changes within a relationship, and the insights that one or both can have there contribute to the overall goal, the assignments that a therapist gives and the work the couple does between sessions make the real difference in the outcome.

- You must be willing to "put your shoulder" to the task and do the homework and follow prescribed recommendations. Sometimes I'll ask a couple, "Have you had any significant conversations since our last session?" When they answer, "No, we have not talked at all," that signals they may not have their marriage problems as a priority. This could result in a difficult task in turning the marriage around.

- Cooperate with the therapist. Sometimes one partner tries to lead the agenda, making sure that it comes out in his/her favor. If you have strong objections to the therapist's style or activities, it would be best to find another therapist with whom you feel more in synch.

- Therapy works best when both partners come willingly and have similar goals. Sometimes one partner has coaxed (threatened, delivered an ultimatum, etc.) the other into coming. That partner may be present in body only and not participate in the interaction. One may want to continue the marriage, and the other has the Exit sign in sight.

- Keep the focus on yourself rather than blaming your partner. Avoid trying to convince the therapist that you are the "golden one" in the marriage.

- Become a part of the team with the therapist. Therapists may have different styles and do different activities with a couple, but all ask themselves, "How can I help this troubled couple?" Better results happen when all parties, therapist and their clients, have their focus on a common goal.

A typical call from a prospective client might sound like this:

"Hello, Ms. Peters?"
"Yes?"
"My insurance company gave me your name, and I would like to make an appointment for couples counseling. My husband and I have been having problems for the past three years, and I have asked him to go to

counseling, but he refused. He seemed to be quite surprised and said he didn't think our situation was bad enough to warrant counseling. Now that I have asked for a separation, he has agreed to come with me."

"So am I to understand that you are willing to work on the marriage then?" I might ask her.

"Well I don't know. If our problems could be resolved, then I would certainly consider it, but I am not hopeful."

Her answer is typical of many, indicating her uncertainty that counseling could help.

I offer this sample phone call to show the extremes encountered in working with couples who wait until the eleventh hour. Many of my clients appear this way, wanting that last desperate effort to save their marriage. I don't have a crystal ball to predict the future, but I do know this: the earlier a couple comes to counseling, the higher the chance of a positive outcome. One of my hopes in writing this book is to sound the warning for early intervention.

What actually happens in therapy?

The clients are able to say important things they have felt afraid to say or didn't know how to say. Often one partner will respond, "I didn't know you felt that way," or "This is the first time I've heard that bothered you." As individuals unload frustrations and resentments, they can then be more open to hearing the needs of their significant other.

Individuals may then get perspective on how the other feels or sees the situation. A change in perspective can lead to a change in attitude, leading to a change in behavior.

In the presence of a neutral moderator/mediator, many partners speak more civilly to their mates, thus making progress in resolving their issues. At home, they may have yelled at each other, increasing the hostility level. In sessions, they may clarify their goals and work on compromise and negotiation. Many individuals don't know how to make requests of their partners; rather, they complain. However, in counseling, couples can start making clear requests of each other.

Therapists teach skills, such as how to communicate more effectively. They often teach partners how to make their needs known more clearly. Before, one may have hinted or expected the other to read his/her mind, or might not have expressed any need in any way. Therapists may help clients resolve baggage they brought into the marriage, either from their families of origin, ex-spouses, etc.

When a couple comes to their first counseling session, I ask questions to get a picture of what the relationship looked like in the beginning. Typical questions are:

- What was it like when you were dating?
- How did he propose?
- What was it like on your wedding day?
- What kinds of feelings did you have on your honeymoon?

How a couple views their past indicates if they still have a fondness and admiration for each other and provides a prognosis for working the marriage out. Obviously if they don't have positive memories there is less of a chance for marital satisfaction in the future. Author and counselor John Gottman says that 94% of the time couples had positive memories, they were likely to have a happy future.

At the end of a session, I usually give only one piece of homework - "The Miracle Question" - that comes from Gurman and Jacobson's book, *The Clinical Handbook of Couples Therapy*. It goes like this:

Suppose when you go home tonight and go to sleep, a miracle happens and the problems that brought you here are solved. But, because you are asleep, you don't know this miracle has happened. So tomorrow, when you wake up and go through your day, you notice things are different between you, but you don't know the miracle happened.

1. What will be the first things you notice are different?
2. What will you notice your partner doing differently that will tell you something has changed?
3. What will your partner notice you doing differently?
4. How will the two of you know you have solved the problems that bring you here or have reached your goals?
5. What will be the first signs (smallest steps) that will tell you that you two are moving in that direction?

The Miracle Question is designed to bring the couple to where they ultimately want to be with each other and to identify achievable and observable goals, the key to a solution-focused model. The assignment is done individually, and then brought to the next session where the couple shares it with one another.

An important point to always remember is that you can't change your spouse. The only person you are capable of changing is yourself.

Some Extra Thought: Relationship Maintenance

Counseling is also helpful for the healthy marriage. Life brings with it many daily challenges, and it's important to keep the focus positive. In a recent session, a woman was talking about the changes she seemed to be making in her marriage. She said that things were improving and she was a lot happier with her husband. When I asked her to pinpoint the cause she called it just "relationship maintenance." I asked for further explanation and she said, "I'm doing the little things that I know are important to my husband and getting good results." She summed it up by saying, "I am focusing on what I *do* have and not on what is missing."

I started to think about the word maintenance, and how it impacts peoples' lives. I wondered if other people believed that their relationships needed maintaining or that they could just take care of themselves. Could many relationship problems be a result of low to zero maintenance from the involved parties?

It occurred to me that many aspects of our daily existence require some sort of maintenance. If we own a car, we all know about the "Factory Scheduled Maintenance Program" that is designed to help ensure trouble-free operation of the car. Following recommended service performed within specific mileage intervals helps anticipate needed repairs and prevent damage from normal wear and tear.

For those who own homes, there are things we need to pay attention to in order to keep a home structurally sound and free from damage by the environment. There are preventive programs, such as monthly termite control, annual air conditioning and heating system checks, fire and smoke detector checks, weekly lawn care and many other items requiring our attention on some regular basis.

What about our health? There are things we need to do to maintain a quality of life. The media floods us with commercials and advertisements about vitamins, herbs, antioxidants, and exercise to keep us in shape and free from disease. The focus is to prevent stress from taking a toll on our bodies.

Maintenance is a household word. Now, when it comes to relationships, where do we stand? Do we have a regular scheduled maintenance plan designed to prevent problems from occurring? While it may not be as simple as a regular scheduled oil change, neglecting it could have similar consequences.

Becoming more attentive to your relationship will contribute to its happiness and longevity. A simple suggestion might be to have a talk with your spouse or partner to find out his/her thoughts on this idea. Then begin to discuss your own individualized maintenance plan. Taking an inventory of what is and isn't working can help to get a jump-start on resolving some issues before they turn into unsolvable ones. A counselor could assist and provide input in this process.

The final step is to realize it's all about choices. To decide to maintain or not is ultimately up to you.

"In love, the paradox occurs that two beings become one and yet remain two."

~ Erich Fromm

Chapter Four

When a Vow Is Taken, a New Life Begins

In a traditional wedding vow, a man takes his wife for better or worse; richer or poorer; in sickness or health; to love and cherish until they part in death. The wife makes the same pledge to her husband. This marks the beginning of their new life together and carries with it the serious task of maintaining an intimate long-term marriage. In order to beat the odds, which are in favor of divorce, you must be willing to not only "talk the talk," but more importantly, "walk the walk."

Although I will be talking about couples in crisis, it is from their struggles that I have found the essential components needed to ensure a lasting, fulfilling marriage. Without these situations, it would not have been possible to write this book.

In a rapidly changing world, relationships today face new problems. Values and commitments are more difficult to keep. Solutions to problems are more complex and need more creative resolutions. Most people are looking for someone to make them happy instead of realizing they must be happy with themselves before they can be happy in a relationship. It is so easy to blame a partner for a failed relationship. No one really wants to take the responsibility of looking inside to ask, "Why?"

I hope you will see the benefits that counseling can offer if you find yourself in an unsatisfactory relationship. In this field, time is of the essence, and success is often closely related to how soon a couple decides to take action. If there is a long time lapse from the beginning of a problem to the beginning of the resolution, problems can grow and cause great distancing. One of the downfalls in couples counseling comes when the couples wait until the problems have reached a critical point. It will take more work to put the relationship back together.

We could compare that situation to more concrete, physical situations: picture a highway that is neglected and abused for a long time - much more repair work will have to be done to restore the highway to a functioning condition.

Let's take a look first at the differences between men and women, as John Gray so aptly states it in *Men are from Mars, Women are from Venus*. Gray very cleverly and accurately describes how the differences between the sexes can influence the quality of their loving relationships.

I always ask couples in counseling to read Gray's book together, as an assignment. The assignment always brings favorable feedback as the couple gains insight into the complexities of their individual personalities and learns how to negotiate their differences through improved communication. In the book, Gray cites the primary love needs of women and men, and discusses the differences.

According to Gray, women need to receive:

Caring	Understanding	Respect
Devotion	Validation	Reassurance

According to Gray, men need to receive:

Trust	Acceptance	Appreciation
Admiration	Approval	Encouragement

Gray emphasizes that, while each needs the other requirements also, the six primary requirements must be met before the others can be fully appreciated. He goes on to state that all twelve kinds of love are ultimately needed by both. Men and women are truly different in many ways. Reading Gray's book will show you some of those differences.

I agree with Gray on many points and find his book well worth reading. In addition to his categories of needs, I also cover other differences with my clients, mainly ones that can cause division between partners. These differences include genetic background, cultural differences, and religious preferences.

Significant differences between spouses and partners in any of the above categories can cause stress that must be managed effectively if the relationship will survive. Is it any wonder - given all the possibilities for being at odds - that the stage is set for conflict? The relationship goes awry when the expectation for success is perfection. Let's look in depth at some of these differences.

Genetic Background

We cannot help our genes. We are born with them, and they aren't going to change. They give us certain attributes that make us unique. We are still learning much about genealogy and finding new gene markers. Since many of the factors that determine our health are inherited, researchers are continually trying to find new links to genetic make-up.

As an example, a growing body of scientific evidence says alcoholism has a genetic link, but researchers have not yet identified an actual gene. Researchers are continuing to study this and look for the genetic causes of alcoholism.

In another field, Behavior Genetics, researchers say that all personality traits have both biological and environmental components. They do say that currently there is no single gene for personality traits or behavior, but that these are influenced by multiple genes.

Cultural Differences

This one can be quite challenging. One's culture defines priorities, understanding of history, psychology, and even the language used. Take, for example, the cultural differences between two individuals raised in different parts of the country.

Think about a southern gentleman teaming up with a New York princess. Can you get a picture of what could go on there? It could be the second Civil War. I say Civil War, but there may be nothing civil about it. A southern gentleman would call it, "The War Between the States" or "The War of Northern Aggression." We all know who won the war, so imagine how that dispute might be handled by this couple.

They actually speak different languages, as well: "Yes ma'am" is not a northern term; neither is "y'all." Aside from the actual words, there is a clear difference in expectations. For example, when a restaurant meal is not satisfactory to the New York lady, she sends it back and requests another. The southern gentleman might rather eat it than be confrontational. The New York lady may speak louder and faster, may walk and talk in a faster way, and may be able to handle multiple tasks. The southern gentleman, on the other hand, may speak with a slow and soft drawl; may behave in a non-confrontational manner; and may be polite to all and never hurry.

The relationship can work, but it surely adds another dimension to the mix. Handling disagreements between the northerner and the southerner is indeed a challenge. For this couple, the cultural differences between them may cause some of their problems.

Religious Preferences
Someone's religion is part of their culture, so the two fields are related. Often it is not a religious preference, but the religion in which a person was raised that can contribute to conflict. Suppose a Catholic man marries a Jewish lady. Now let's add the geographically diverse background to the mix, and say it is the couple above from the north and south. Do the problems intensify? Yes, they will, and we still have not gotten to the list of common problems that usually bring couples to counseling.

If a Baptist lady marries a Catholic gentleman, she will be asked to raise her children in the Catholic Church. Does she know enough about the religion to agree to this? One should study the partner's religion to know if it is agreeable to him or her.

Other factors I have not described can have huge influences on a marriage. Suppose one partner has been raised in luxury while the other one was raised on food stamps. Suppose one was the oldest child in the family and had the responsibility of younger siblings, and the other was the baby of the family who was cared for like royalty. I suppose by now you might be asking yourself: with all those differences, how does anyone make a marriage that lasts a lifetime?

There are many problems for which a couple might seek counseling. I will list some and then go on to review the more prominent ones in depth. By using some examples from real life cases, it may seem like I am talking about you or someone you know. Although some of the situations in this book are real, identities or any real cases have been changed to protect confidentiality. Their conflicts and resolutions are used to demonstrate the complexity of relationships today. These are some of the common problems my clients face:

Alcohol/drug abuse
Blended families
Communication
Infidelity
Depression/anxiety of one spouse (or both)
Financial conflict
Life-changing events (such as a death of a child)
Emotional abuse
Parenting conflicts
Sexual addictions
Work/job stress

These are not inclusive but target a good proportion of the problem areas. Some couples may have multiple issues going on simultaneously, creating a more difficult case.

Know the FACTS

Given all the differences noted in my experiences with couples, I have discovered five elements that are essential to the success of all good relationships. I call these the FACTS.

F is for forgiveness
A is for acceptance
C is for compassion
T is for trust
S is for spirituality

In the next few chapters, we will examine the FACTS to illuminate the actions, habits, and attitudes that are key to a successful relationship.

Some Extra Thought Considering Divorce

If you do get a divorce, the days ahead may be difficult. All of the things you shared with your partner, such as eating meals together; raising children together; sharing chores, finances, family holidays, vacations and friends will be gone forever. In addition, you will have lost the intimacy and close friendship that you had with your significant other.

Divorce is like a death in the way that it changes people's lives and requires a grieving process for the loss. Not only will you be depriving your children of a loving, two-parent family, but you will be depriving yourself of the person who has been the closest to you in life. Most people say they left their marriage due to the constant stress, and only wind up suffering more stress because they weren't prepared for the emotional aspects of dissolving a marriage.

Divorce carries with it emotional and physical health problems. In fact, statistics say that the risk of suicide is greater for people going through divorce. You become more susceptible to psychiatric problems such as depression and anxiety. All relationships change and you find yourself in an emotional quandary trying to keep friends and family connected.

Sometimes divorce is necessary if the relationship is abusive and destructive to the family, and the other person is not open to receiving help in order to improve the situation. It is better to separate only after you have made every possible effort on your part, and when you see that resolution is not possible.

"If we really want to love, we must learn how to forgive."

~ Mother Theresa

Chapter Five

F Is for Forgiveness

Forgiveness plays a significant role in all human relationships. The following case comes to mind in which the husband recently confessed to having had an affair. Although he said it was over, the wife felt the need to seek counseling. At that time, she wanted to continue the marriage, but she did not want to be vulnerable to that type of hurt ever again. Although he tried very hard on his part to do the right things, she had a lot of trouble forgiving him because she continued going over the affair in her mind and could not understand the reasons for his actions. She did not know if he saw his part in it very clearly, nor was she confident that he would always be faithful in the future.

G. and M.

G. and her husband, M., appeared very anxious when they walked into my office. They sat at opposite ends of the couch and avoided eye contact with each other.

G. talked first. "M. and I have been married for fifteen years. We have always gotten along really well, and we have two lovely children. A few weeks ago, I noticed he was spending a lot of time on his cell phone. Even late at night, I would see him out on the porch talking on it. When I asked whom he was talking to, he simply said it was one of the guys from his work.

"A few days later, I saw M. leaving a restaurant with a woman I had never seen before. They were talking and laughing, and then they both got into her car.

"I went home, and when M. got home later that night, I didn't know what to do. After the kids were asleep, I decided to question him. He tried to explain the lunch date was for business and said that everything was fine. I guess I should have been more aware of his behavior, but being a stay-at-home mom, I was always so preoccupied with the kids.

We never seemed to spend much time together anymore. When we did spend time together, we always did something for the kids.

"That night after M. had gone to sleep, I slipped his cell phone from the nightstand, went downstairs, and checked the numbers. He had gotten lots of calls from one number, so I called it on his phone. A female answered. I quickly hung up, but I know she recognized the number because she answered, 'Hi, honey.'

"Needless to say, I was furious. My heart started racing, my hands got cold, and I was shaking for a moment or two. I knew I had to pull myself together because of the kids. I confronted my husband, and he no longer denied that everything was fine. He said that he would end the affair, that he was sorry, and that he would do anything to fix our marriage. He said that he loved me and our family."

For M., it was quite difficult for him to confess to G. He was afraid of what she would say or do. He told his story like this: "I was afraid, but I knew I had to come clean. Besides, it was a stupid thing to do, and I knew better. I just don't know how I let myself get carried away. I really am mad at myself for causing so much trouble for our family. I wish I could make it go away. I am very sorry and want to make it up to her. I love my wife, and always have, ever since we met in college. But, after the children came, they became her life. She is so involved with the kids, taking them to all kinds of lessons, helping with schoolwork, and socializing with her friends and their kids, that I just don't seem to be important anymore.

"I know that is not an excuse for my behavior. It was easy to fall for attention from someone else. The only problem was that it went too far. I didn't know how to ask my wife for what I needed. We have a history together, and I now know how special it is. I hope it is not too late for us."

Honesty and confession was a good starting point for both of them. I began by asking some pertinent questions so that we could formulate a plan to get them back on track.

How do you want me to help?
What was your relationship like before you had children?
What was involved in your decision to have children? Was it a mutual one or did one need to convince the other?
What were your expectations regarding families with children?

I also asked how they typically communicated their needs to each other. To G., I asked if she was aware of M.'s need for attention. To M., I asked if he was having a hard time sharing G. with the children.

Here are some basic things to consider in M. and G.'s situation. There has been a breach of trust, a deception, and a reaching out for needs that are not met in the marital relationship. First and foremost, there is a need to recommit and to reclaim their place within the marriage. An affair doesn't have to mean the end of a relationship. Sometimes it can be the beginning of a better one. While I do many different things with a couple dealing with an affair, in this chapter, I focus on forgiveness.

First I said to M., "You must openly admit your involvement and understand the nature of your actions. You must state that you take full responsibility and apologize for the pain you caused G."

M. and G. needed to learn how to forgive. It is from the point of forgiveness that healing can take place.

After we spent time talking through their history, from both sides, and they were completely satisfied with moving on, we shifted the focus to forgiveness. I said to G., "You must be able to find a way to forgive M.'s behavior." G.'s holding onto resentment would block the healing of the relationship and hurt G. herself. G. needed to avail herself of the benefits that come from forgiving.

To M., I said, "You must be able to forgive yourself for your own actions and for the hurt you caused."

When I talk about forgiveness with a couple who has come to counseling for a breach in trust, perhaps because of an affair, they immediately think that I am asking one to accept or excuse the inappropriate or wrong behavior of the other. That is a common misunderstanding and warrants clarification. Forgiveness is not about having to pretend that someone didn't hurt you.

What I mean is that one needs to forgive the other so that they can move forward with the relationship and begin to accept the new behavior without continually looking back on the old. It doesn't mean that the offended person continues to allow the other person to hurt him or her. Forgiveness says "what you did hurt me, but I choose to forgive you for my own sake."

Forgiving doesn't mean that M.'s behavior becomes null and void or that it becomes pardoned. It means that G. finds a place to realize the flaws in the human condition and sees it as an opportunity to find out what was missing in the relationship that allowed this transgression. It is an opportunity for them to get closer.

The couple will need encouragement and support from each other as they try to reclaim their vows. As they forgive each other, they must learn to forgive themselves for past mistakes and transgressions.

I often find that couples aren't even able to define forgiveness and therefore have little experience with how to start.

Forgiveness is a process that goes against the aspect of human nature that seeks revenge. It often requires the help of a friend, a clergy member, or a counselor. Time should be spent in defining forgiveness adequately.

The concept and benefits of forgiveness have been explored in religions, the social sciences, and medicine. Forgiveness may be considered simply in terms of the person who forgives, in terms of the person forgiven, and in terms of the relationship between the forgiver and the forgiven. In some cases, forgiveness may be granted without any compensation or any response on the part of the offender. In the Bible, the Parable of the Prodigal Son gives a well-known instance of religious teachings and the practice of forgiveness.

We all have memories. Some are happy and some are sad. We often keep our memories in photograph books and scrapbooks, but these are usually the happy memories. Often we harbor memories of hurt feelings and wrongs that have been committed against us. Many have reported sleepless nights remembering some hurtful score from the past. One might say, "I forgave him for what he did, but I'll never forget it." Emotional garbage will always clutter that person's head.

When we truly forgive a person, we must try to forget the transgression also. People make mistakes every day, especially in a marriage. If the partners start keeping a tally of those mistakes, they become like a heavy knapsack on their backs, and they can grow bent from the weight of it. Naturally, healing from a genuine wrongdoing by another takes time; it can help the hurt to focus on forgiveness and forgetting and stop reliving the hurt in the mind. We cannot love unless we learn to forgive.

Always be willing and ready to say the words, "I'm sorry." Sometimes they seem like the two hardest words in the language to say, but nothing can be more healing than those two words when the offender is truly repentant.

No one, and no marriage, is - or ever will be - perfect. Just like life, human beings are a work in progress. If you have a hurtful argument with your spouse, time works against you if you remain angry. Holding onto anger causes it to turn into resentment, which is debilitating to any relationship. Be quick to resolve it. Never go to bed angry or holding a grudge. Sometimes it may be necessary to schedule a conversation for a later time if one is sick or too tired to talk that night, but a couple must always be thinking ahead to the resolution of a dispute.

Forgiveness lets you put the past behind you. There are many levels of forgiveness in a relationship, and we forgive in some aspect every day of our lives with someone close to us. We may forgive a small act, such as a spouse not taking out the trash when asked, or not taking the dog out, or children not cleaning up their rooms when asked. Our forgiving is probably unconscious in these respects, and we move beyond the being angry part quickly.

A significant part of our view of forgiveness comes from our family of origin: how we were taught and what we saw about forgiveness shaped our feelings and behavior. Maybe we came from a family where once a wrong behavior occurred it was written in stone and no kind of apology was sufficient. Maybe we saw anger and pain rather than unconditional love and acceptance where mistakes can be allowed. Recognizing the flawed nature of our existence helps keep the perspective that we are not perfect and do not live in a perfect world.

As Scott Peck writes in *The Road Less Traveled*, "Life is difficult but once you realize that life is difficult . . . it is no longer difficult." Once you can accept the flawed nature of people, it becomes easier to forgive.

Larry James offers this prayer about forgiveness: "Living, loving Presence, I enter this moment of silence and consciously make the decision to unburden and detach myself from the painful memories of the past. I release to you everything that holds me back from my spiritual journey. I feel your power working in and through me in forgiving and letting go all that needs to be forgiven and released. And so it is."

Some Extra Thought: The Benefits of Forgiveness

Oscar Wilde advised, "Forgive your enemies; nothing annoys them so much."

In the article, "Forgive and Let Live" in *Newsweek* in 2004, the following information confirms the benefit of forgiveness. Researchers and doctors show that the act of forgiveness is good for you. Scientists are interested in the health benefits of forgiveness. Their studies show the emotional, physical and mental side effects of unforgiving thoughts. In the clinical psychology field, there are more than 1200 published studies in 2009, compared with only 58 back in 1997.

According to Dr. Everet Worthington Jr., a professor at Virginia Commonwealth University and Executive Director of the Campaign for Forgiveness Research, every time you withhold forgiving, you are more likely to develop a health problem. Worthington distinguishes what he calls "decisional forgiveness" - a commitment to reconcile with the perpetrator - from the more significant "emotional forgiveness, an internal state of forgiveness." Some of the health benefits of forgiveness are:

Lower blood pressure
Improved immune system
Decreased anxiety and depression
Improved sleep
Improved self esteem and gives a sense of empowerment
More rewarding relationships
Reduced stress
Increased energy

Sometimes the forgiveness demonstrated by unique cultural or religious groups can awe us. I was moved to tears when I read about the terrible murders of six Amish children by Charles Carl Roberts in Pennsylvania in 2006. The Amish community forgave this man who had murdered their children and went on to offer his wife their condolences. Most of us aren't able to penetrate that level of forgiveness or separate the act from the person. It is a very difficult thing to do.

Another part of forgiveness is self-forgiveness. We need to be able to look at ourselves in a mirror and see the imperfections and choose to forgive our transgressions. We need to judge ourselves on ourselves and not on our behavior, good or bad. If we aren't able to forgive ourselves, it will certainly be hard to forgive others.

The word forgiveness is built on the root word give. Give yourself the gift of forgiveness. It releases your partner from your criticism and also releases you from being imprisoned by your own negative judgment. It releases the poison from your body and lets you live again. Forgiveness is the key to your own happiness. Forgiving someone else takes moral courage. It ends the illusion of separation, and its power can change misery into happiness in an instant. Forgiveness means choosing to let go, move on and favor the positive.

~Larry James

"God grant me the serenity to accept the things I cannot change; courage to change the things I can; and wisdom to know the difference."

~ Reinhold Niebuhr

Chapter Six

A Is for Acceptance

Following are some of the new insights that Rick Warren, author of *A Purpose Driven Life* and pastor of Saddleback Church in California, had about acceptance after his wife contracted cancer and he achieved wealth from the book sales.

In an interview by Jim Dailey of *Decision Magazine*, a publication by the Billy Graham Evangelical Association, Rick revealed how he felt about that year. Although he had tremendous success with his book, he was also aiding his wife through a very difficult battle with cancer. (As of this writing, she is in remission.) His family had also been struggling for years with the mental illness of his son, who eventually took his own life, a decade after this interview. Rick talked about life's difficulties: "Rather than life being hills and valleys, I believe that it's kind of like two rails on a railroad track, and at all times you have something good and something bad in your life. No matter how good things are in your life, there is always something bad that needs to be worked on. And no matter how bad things are in your life, there is always something good.

You can focus on your purposes, or you can focus on your problems. If you focus on your problems, you're going into self-centeredness, which is my problem, my issues, my pain. But one of the easiest ways to get rid of pain is to get your focus off yourself and onto God and others."

You have to learn to deal with both the good and the bad of life.

Couples must accept each other for what they are if they are to have a successful marriage. Every couple will - sooner or later - need to accept some irritating behavior or personality characteristic of the partner. It gets more complicated when there is a blended family: where second or third marriages incorporate children from two families living together. Acceptance of differences becomes critical and challenging.

Every person brings his/her past to the marriage. In a second marriage, acceptance plays an especially big role. Since each has been married before, each brings additional challenges from their previous relationships along with their own childhood dynamics. There is also the element of a failed marriage, and possible fears of yet another disaster.

When one or both bring children into the new marriage, the need for acceptance reaches new levels that now encompass each other's children. Parenting skills become crucial. Each partner must accept the other for who they are and what they believe, and then they are able to incorporate the best measures of each into their blended family dynamics. There must be a commitment to work cooperatively on raising the children.

L. and R.

The following is an example of a couple whose situation required a great deal of acceptance. I observed at our first counseling session that L. was in her early thirties and wore her hair in a long red ponytail. She was pregnant and wearing a loose fitting shirt. Her blonde, blue-eyed husband, R., had the stubble of a beard and was wearing a University of Georgia sweatshirt.

L. said, "We both have two children - each from our previous marriages, and we are expecting our first child together. My children live with us, and his two are here on weekends and most of the summer vacation. But, our children don't get along. It is a constant fight the whole time his children are here, and R. sides with his kids, which causes us to argue. He is good to my children except when his kids are with us. A large portion of our income goes to his ex-wife to support his kids. I get some child support and use it for my kids, but when his children are here a lot of it has to go for his kids, too.

We are now adding a new baby to the mix. Seeing how R. acts with his kids, I know he is going to put this baby and its needs ahead of my kids' needs all the time. We will be constantly arguing over money and everything else. I'm thinking about taking my children and my unborn baby and just leaving and starting over."

R. had his version of the story as well. "We see L.'s kids every day, but mine are only over on the weekends. L. acts like she resents me for giving them extra attention, and wanting to do things with them. We are going to have a new baby and I'm real happy about that, but I'm afraid that once the baby is here, L. will shut my kids out completely. I love my children and they must be treated equal. If my children aren't happy, then I'm not happy."

Blended families are becoming more and more common - yours, mine and ours - and it does take some adjustments to get things on an even ground. The fact that couples have children from previous marriages is a fact that they cannot change. The fact they love their children from a previous marriage is something they don't want to change. Of course, both will love the children they have together.

A good way to look at a blended family is: suppose you are making a cake from scratch, and each member of the family is one of the ingredients. Each ingredient has something special to offer, and if one of the ingredients is missing, then the cake will be bad - or at least not as good. It is by the blending of these ingredients and the proper nurturing while allowing the cake to cook and cool that makes the perfect dessert.

In this case, L. felt anxious about bringing a new baby into the family without some good communication of how they would give equal attention to all. Children are really very smart and know which buttons to push for attention. Without setting good limits across the board and being on the same page with discipline, confusion is inevitable.

Clearly the first problem for L. and R. was communication. Communicating is one of the essential elements of a satisfying relationship. It is always a prevalent factor in all the couples I have seen. It is important to know what the expectations are of each other instead of assuming or denying that there are any. In a relationship, one does not operate in a vacuum. So both people need to be open and honest about how they want to see things done and then work on compromising until an acceptable approach is reached.

A good technique for couples to use is called mirroring or reflective listening. The listener tries to clarify and restate or paraphrase what the other person is saying. For example: The listener says: "So what you are saying is ...;" or "Let me see if I got that right. You want ...." The listener sends the information back without analysis, judgment or opinion, just the facts as she or he heard them. Then the speaker can either confirm or deny what the other person heard. The couple repeats this process until each spouse clearly understands the semantic and emotional content of the other person's statement. There is no mistake as to what the other is asking or stating as both people agree on the request or complaint.

The second part then becomes the validating and empathizing.

That might sound like this: "That makes sense to me . . ." validates.

"Given all of that, I'd imagine you are feeling . . ." empathizes.

When this is used properly, there is tremendous satisfaction for the sender knowing that his or her message was received exactly as intended. The sender also gets feedback, which enables further conversation to continue progressing to a fulfilling dialogue. This process is timely in teaching, as it is not comfortable in the beginning and requires practice to perfect it.

Due to the benefits of mirroring, I often use it with my couples. It avoids the cycle of criticism, blame, and defensiveness that is often the most destructive pattern of communication.

So for L. and R., they first need to inform each other of their fears or concerns in a manner that can be understood. At that point, we move into negotiation of the new approach with the kids. We review some of their own parenting from their own parents and then see how they have brought those ideas into their current marriage.

With L. and R., both must try to get away from the concept of "yours and mine" and think now only of "ours." They must think of all the children as "ours." L. must accept R.'s children as if they are her own, and he must do the same for hers. The baby, of course, will be "theirs," and all the children must be accepted for who they are and all treated equally. They must accept their family as a unit and be accepting of all the likenesses and differences. Above all, they must regard their relationship as a top priority and not allow the children to set the rules. Consistency in this type of family is crucial to its success. There is no margin of error because the children can make or break this union.

With L. and R., as with other couples, as they continued to come in for weekly sessions, they learned more about themselves and each other. Couples, including L. and R., then become more accepting of themselves and of their spouses. They realize what they want to work on to change about their own personalities. They work on accepting the other person for who she or he is and to appreciate the fact that the other person is trying to make changes in their behavior. They learn to ask for what they want and also practice putting themselves in their partners' shoes.

A good friend of mine said this about her marriage:

"What I believe to be the one reason that my husband and I share a successful relationship is due to our respect for each other as individuals - albeit with different interests and unique needs. We have allowed each other the freedom to be ourselves. In addition, over the forty-two years that we have been married, it has been evident that both of us have had the same vision for our future. There is a saying, 'Love consists not merely in gazing at one another, but rather in looking out in the same direction.' I believe this to be very true."

The serenity prayer used in AA has often led alcoholics to accept the fact they are alcoholics while learning to live a productive life in spite of it. The prayer applies not only to alcoholics, but to all of us who must accept the things in life we cannot change.

One mistake couples often make is marrying a person, and thinking that the other will change. Changing someone else is usually impossible. But yet the quest goes on. There is a false sense of power that leads many people to believe that they can get their spouse to act differently, but ultimately it begins a process of frustration and disappointment.

This is worth repeating: You must accept a person for who he or she is. The only person you can change is yourself, and often even that requires hard work. People get comfortable in their own skins and sometimes keeping old behaviors becomes more secure than venturing out into new water. One sad reason that people stay in bad marriages is because they have become too comfortable with the way things are and fear what is unknown. In the following situation, one spouse believed that the other spouse's behavior would change once they were married.

J. and H.

J. and H. were married for almost four years before attending counseling. H. was J.'s first husband, but he had been married before. His first wife divorced him because he was an alcoholic. But, after they divorced he went to AA and stopped drinking. He said he would never drink again and that he drank from unhappiness in his first marriage.

J.'s mother believed, "Once an alcoholic, always an alcoholic." J.'s grandfather was an alcoholic, but her grandmother stayed with him, and they had a miserable life. Because of that, she didn't want J. to marry H., but J. believed that H. had changed his drinking behavior.

J. and H. had been happy, especially since their daughter had been born two years ago. But about two months before counseling began, H. started coming home from work late, and J. could smell alcohol on his breath, and in his skin.

H. said he and his buddies just stopped off to have some beers. J. asked him not to do that, reminding him of his former problem with alcohol. But, he was still doing it. It had gone from once a week to almost every night. It didn't stop even after she threatened to leave him.

J. loves H., and they both adore their daughter. H. doesn't want J. to leave and said he would try counseling.

At our first session, H. told his story like this:

"I work all week and I want to stop off with the guys and have a few beers. I like the taste of beer; besides, the guys are going to rib you if you say you want a soda.

"J. can go out with her friends during the day while I'm working, and her mother keeps our daughter. I take J. out every Saturday. She doesn't let me have a drink when we go out, and I don't have any alcohol in the house because she doesn't want it around our daughter. I'm fine with that, but I work hard, and I deserve a little fun without her getting freaked out and threatening to leave me."

Often we get clues from our past that can help us work out the present. At that time, I began the process of obtaining family information from H. I found out there was significant alcohol family dynamics. I also learned that J.'s family had a history with alcohol as well. I found out that H. had briefly attended AA, had two previous DUI's, and some job-related problems due to his drinking.

The first challenge they faced was H.'s denial. In H.'s mind, he saw the failure of his first marriage as the cause of his drinking, when it probably was the drinking that caused the marriage to end. H. never did admit to being an alcoholic, and it would be necessary to do a thorough alcohol and drug evaluation to make that diagnosis.

However, enough information was obtained from just speaking with them to make a "probable diagnosis." I would make a referral to another counselor who was qualified to handle this type of situation, and provide the necessary treatment.

But at the time of our first meeting, I offered the following information based on what they had provided. Alcoholics have a difficult time accepting their disease and tend to externalize and blame everyone else for the reason they drink (i.e. a failing marriage). The first step was for H. to acknowledge his denial, and to realize that alcoholism is a disease and not reversible. He needed to make a decision to give up drinking and save his marriage, or it, too, would probably end the same way the first one did. The problem had intensified because he had a second wife with the same complaints.

J.'s needs were twofold. First she needed to understand the dynamics of the disease and fully accept the road ahead as challenging. She had to make the decision to accept H. with this problem and make the best of their marriage. She had to realize that relapse is common and may occur several times in the future. J. also needed to learn the difference between enabling and supportive behavior to best deal with H.'s drinking.

Second, J. needed to take care of herself in the process, and attend Al-Anon meetings for support and understanding of her alcoholic spouse's behavior. Getting involved with a support group would give J. an outlet for her to express feelings in a supportive environment.

In this situation, marriage counseling needs to be structured and criteria needs to be put in place. It is best if the alcoholic is attending individual or group treatment for his issues of recovery and is no longer drinking. It is also beneficial for the spouse to be attending support concurrently. As alcohol has become a family disease, now there is a focus on sobriety, improved communication, and an acceptance of the path of recovery. Each partner can address the impact that alcohol is having on the relationship and engage in problem solving to address ways the relationship will need to change when the alcohol is reduced or eliminated.

Without a sincere commitment to abstain from alcohol, this couple would have had a bleak future. Alcohol might have become the relationship of choice for H., and J. would become second to John's drinking. H. needed to give up his addiction and put his love into his spouse. Whenever there is an addiction, it becomes primary, and everything else is reduced to second. They both have alcoholic histories and faced a difficult road. For success in this case, sobriety was crucial. Often many counselors for couples would not begin counseling until the person was in treatment and free of alcohol. Most addictions cause similar relationship problems and intensify the treatment options.

Because of their love for each and for their daughter, J. and H. were able to save their marriage. Both J. and H. faced the fact that H. was alcoholic, and they both proceeded to get some help for him. They must accept the fact that H. will always be an alcoholic, but with love, faith, and patience they can overcome alcohol abuse and have a satisfying relationship.

Sometimes it is difficult to accept others as they are, because we have not made peace with who we are. As children we may have been subjected to criticism by adults who mean well, but don't understand a child's feelings. Maybe we think our nose is too big or we are overweight. Cosmetic surgery may be able to change some things, but we can't change the color of our skin; who our relatives are; or disabilities that we were born with. We have all faced the pain of not measuring up to an imposed ideal, but it is important to accept yourself as you are before you can accept others for who they are.

Some Extra Thought: Perfect Your Skills of Acceptance

Learn not to criticize. Ridiculing your mate for behavior you do not accept will not make the other change. It will only make the problem grow. Focus on your mate's strong qualities and behaviors, and praise him/her for these and tell them they have so many strong points, you know they will be able to improve the others.

Be a good listener. Sometimes when a person can talk with his or her spouse and feel that the spouse is really interested in hearing about the problem, just talking allows him or her to figure out the best way to find resolutions.

Think of constructive things you can do together that will help a spouse solve his/her problems.

Humor helps. Laughter is the best medicine, and laughing about a problem sometimes makes it go away. Making fun of yourself in a lighthearted way is a good form of acceptance. Humor reduces stress and adds spice to a relationship.

Have realistic expectations of your mate and your marriage. It is what it is! Your marriage is a work in progress. Accept that. And let time and love take its course.

"Compassion is the ultimate and most meaningful embodiment of emotional maturity. It is through compassion that a person achieves the highest peak and deepest reach in his or her search for self-fulfillment."

~ Arthur Jersild

Chapter Seven

C Is for Compassion

Compassion is tenderness and concern shown to a person in need of caring. It is more than empathy, and carries the desire to alleviate another's suffering. It is a feeling deep within us, a way of acting, affected by the suffering of others. Acting compassionately increases our capacity to care and reinforces charity, empathy, and sympathy. The following couple's story demonstrates the fruit of compassion in marriage.

Y. and T.

Probably one of the most memorable couples I have counseled was Y. and T. – a nice couple in their mid-twenties. In their adapting to and supporting each other through extreme trauma, they demonstrated compassion that eventually strengthened their marriage.

They called because they had just suffered the loss of their adopted daughter, a toddler. They were in despair and were looking for guidance on how to deal with their loss. They came in together and told their story. They had adopted because T. had a genetic problem he did not want to pass on. After Y. and T. had been together for five years, they went to an orphanage overseas. After meeting the little girl in the fall, they brought her home at New Year's and were filled with joy.

Y. did most of the talking as she recounted the traumatic details of their daughter's accidental death. R., their daughter, had hit her head on a table, never to regain consciousness. A family member had been watching the child while Y. was getting rest.

During our initial meeting, they talked about their struggle over adopting a child; and then there were the feelings of guilt, anger, sadness, and helplessness over the loss of a child. They felt responsible; they lost confidence in their parenting and struggled with being angry with God. They reported a fear of moving forward and trusting themselves with another child.

"I think we're lost," Y. said, as she talked about the burial of their daughter.

She was tearful and sobbed, while her husband comforted her. He was looking at her and touching her softly. While T. was also feeling the same emotions, I observed him being totally connected with and providing support to Y.

For Y., the talking was helpful, and for T., his silence was compassionate.

After a year of counseling, they had reached a safe place and were prepared to continue on with their plans to adopt again. Y. had attended a grief support group. Their coping skills were different, and they were allowing each other to grieve in their own way. For Y. it was verbal, for T. it was more quiet and introspective. He reported talking to R. nightly in his thoughts. For Y. it was important to keep the child's room intact and her toys around. They even brought a picture album to share with me as they celebrated her life and their brief time with her.

A few months later, I received a request to write a letter on their behalf to a local adoption agency. With the couple's permission, I agreed and was able to state that I had been privileged to watch this couple progress through the grief process with an amazing ability of compassion for one another. During the five-month period of counseling, they displayed commitment to each other while never wavering in their support of each other. They were able to follow their own needs, giving themselves permission to experience profound grief, while working through guilt, anger, sadness and difficulties with faith. Their relationship soared to a greater level of strength, showing respect, love, and kindness.

I received a "Thank You" card from them stating their appreciation for my experience and for the compassion I had shown them during their time in counseling. When contacting them for permission to use their story in this book, they happily announced that they now have a beautiful son. Their relationship was profound and confirmed for me the necessity of placing compassion as one of the five essential qualities for a lifetime relationship.

Another example of compassion comes from another couple I know. They have been married for more than sixty years. They have a sign over their bed that reads "Always kiss me good night." That means they don't go to bed angry and the hurts of the day are ruled out by love and compassion. One of the basic reasons we marry is to have our needs met. These needs need to be met with compassion.

In a marriage, compassion is crucial. It is easy to show compassion toward a mate when someone close to them dies or if they are in the hospital very sick. But, how about the everyday problems, such as when a wife has had a hard day with the kids? Try a little tenderness. It would be great to offer to watch the kids for a while and let her get a nice bubble bath, or if meal planning is running her crazy, why not get a sitter and take her out to dinner?

Husbands need compassion, too. What if he didn't get the raise he was expecting or if the car started having problems on the way home from work, and he knows the repairs are going to be expensive? Or what if the receptionist at work (who is almost his age) said he reminded her of her father? Why not take a stroll in the park holding hands or give him a nice massage? These little acts of understanding and compassion help cement a relationship.

How to Dance in the Rain

The following story, which has circulated around the Internet in various forms, evidences compassion that binds a couple together, even during a prolonged and terminal illness.

An older woman sat next to me on the bus as I went to work one summer morning. Normally I drive my car, but it was in the shop for repairs. I could tell that she seemed eager to get somewhere at this early hour. I asked her how her morning was going. She said that the morning was going great and that she was meeting her husband. I asked if they were going somewhere special. She said no, that she was going to his nursing home, where he had been for several years with memory loss. I realized suddenly that he might not know her any more. We sat in silence for the next few minutes as the bus lurched on through traffic toward our destinations. As I got ready to get off at the next stop, I told her how wonderful it was that they would have the morning together. "Yes," she said. "He does not recognize me. But I surely do know him."

True love is neither physical, nor romantic. True love is an acceptance of all that is, has been, will be, and will not be. The happiest people don't necessarily have the best of everything; they just make the best of everything they have.

Life isn't about how to survive the storm, but how to dance in the rain.

This beautiful story gives a poignant example of compassion and acceptance. The wife could not change her husband's Alzheimer's disease, and she couldn't change the fact that he no longer recognized her, but she chose to be there for him on a daily basis.

R. and S.

On another level, compassion can be seen in the case of R and S., husband and wife. R. and S. live with S.'s father, F. F. is eighty-nine years old, has a heart condition, and walks with a cane most of the time, but sometimes needs to be in a wheel chair. They have remodeled the house with ramps and other aids so he can get around. S. is F.'s only daughter, and he also has one son. The son and his wife both work, and they have small children, so they would rather give S. money each month and let F. stay with her. They have looked into assisted living, but the nice places cost more than S. can afford - even with her brother's help and F.'s Social Security check.

But, R. is not happy with the living arrangement. He says, "The problem is that F. takes all of my wife's time. She has to wait on him like a baby; he even has a monitor in his room. We can't talk at dinner because she has to help feed him. We can't watch T.V. at night because she is constantly taking him to the bathroom or getting him something. I think he knows when we try to make love at night because he calls her on the monitor every time, and if she doesn't go right away, he starts acting like he is dying. When we go out on weekends, we have to pay a sitter, and usually the sitter will call us four or five times because F. won't cooperate with anyone except my wife. I eat take-out most of the time, as S. doesn't have time to cook because she has been at the doctor's, therapy or the senior center with her father. I told her it was time for a nursing home, but she has refused. One reason is because she promised her mother, before her mother died, that she would look after him. I come second to Daddy, and maybe that sounds childish, but I really need a wife who can be a wife. I love her, but I don't know what to do."

R. persuaded S. to come into counseling. S. wore black pants and a red sweater, long earrings, and had her dark hair up in a French twist. R. wore dress pants and a white dress shirt and had nice blue eyes and dark hair.

I asked S. to tell me how she viewed their living arrangement. "Well, Daddy fell last night," she started. "He didn't get hurt badly, but I had to sit in his room most of the night because it scared him. He likes for me to read to him, too, and I fell asleep doing that last night because I was so tired. His mind is very sharp, but he is not able to do much for himself physically, so he requires a lot of attention. He is my father, and he has always been there for me, so I am going to be there for him. R. doesn't understand because his parents aren't to that point yet, and besides, there are six children in his family who could help in a situation like this. But, Daddy only wants me, and I'm happy to do it. Why can't R. understand that Daddy has only a few years left to live? Then we can go on with our lives. I think it is cruel for him to be so selfish."

51

Since so much of S.'s attention is directed to her father, R. probably feels very much left out and unimportant. For S., it is more complicated. She is trying to do several things at once. Her father's wishes and mother's last request are foremost now and take precedence over all else.

R. needs to be patient, even if it means his needs are not met for a time. But, S. must find compassion for Ralph who is also suffering because he has lost her in the sense that he has to share her more than is reasonable. She must re-affirm her love to R. and ask how she could make it easier for him.

S. needs to try to see the situation as he does. When they both do this, they will each have a better understanding of the other's needs. It will be necessary to communicate often and openly, and to offer support to each other.

Acting compassionately is putting the other person first. It is getting outside of your own needs and into the other's place. It is kind, unselfish, and patient. It is opening your heart, stretching your capacity to care about the other's needs. Married couples can weather difficult times with more ease when they direct a compassionate heart toward each other's needs.

Some Extra Thought: Compassion, Elderly Parents, and Marriage

Since parents are living longer these days, they sometimes become the responsibility of their children. It can often put stress on a marriage.

In an article in *The Atlanta Journal & Constitution* (March 22, 2009) Helen Oliviero writes that caring for aging parents is a life baby boomers know well. Four out of ten are caring for aging parents. A survey by Caring.com, an online source for adult children caring for their parents, found that 80% of 300 baby boomers say taking care of aging parents is putting a big strain on their marriages. Some helpful hints are:

- Find out your parents' wishes and go about the best way of taking care of them.
- Get help. Churches and senior centers offer help.
- Ask siblings, not just for help in general, but to do specific things such as taking care of Dad for one afternoon or taking him to the doctor.
- Take care of yourself. Hire a sitter long enough for a movie or shopping trip.
- Turn it off. Spend an evening with a spouse with no mention of parents or problems with parents.

*"Honesty is hardly ever heard,
but mostly what I need from you."*

~ Billy Joel, "Honesty"

Chapter Eight

T Is for Trust

When trust issues plague a marriage, the couple has a hard time communicating on many levels. Having trust makes one feel safe. Trust is one of the most important factors in relationship dynamics because of the importance of communication. If spouses cannot trust each other, then they cannot communicate effectively about their feelings, their goals, or the health of the relationship.

L. and B.

L. and B. were a young couple in their thirties with four-year-old twin boys. My initial recollection of L. was that she was calm and cool when she talked about setting the appointment for counseling. She and her husband were looking for assistance with a recently discovered affair that her husband had had a year ago with a co-worker.

At our first meeting, they appeared connected to each other and verbalized the same goals. B. stated, "I stepped out of the bounds of our marriage and had an affair for five months with a co-worker." Their stated goal as a couple was to continue to have a healthy, trusting, and loving marriage.

B. also wanted to improve their communication of feelings for each other. He reported feelings of a depressed mood and stress in the past two years. These stressors included relocating from their home in New Jersey to Atlanta due to a job loss, and unresolved medical issues. He had just gone through surgery for removal of his appendix and gallbladder. Currently he was going through a battery of procedures, including a pet scan and a liver biopsy to rule out cancer.

Both B. and L. work outside of the home and equally take care of their twin boys. Most importantly, B. said he loved his wife and didn't know why he strayed from his commitment.

I observed L. to be soft spoken, connected, and supportive to B.

L. stated that she was invested in working it out, and that she was not considering divorce under any circumstance. It seemed too good to be true at the first meeting. My experience in working with couples in their situation has always been more negative and accusatory, so this was quite a refreshing outlook.

L. and B. came to seven couples' sessions. Their homework consisted of list of books to read, communication techniques, forgiveness worksheets, and a lot of "one on one" discussions. We also discussed developing a "Trust Contract." They were willing to keep appointments and complete the homework.

They both had forgiveness issues - L. for B. and B. for himself. In fact, Laura progressed quickly, whereas B. had a harder time. He struggled with guilt and remorse for his actions. L. was able to tell B. what she needed on a daily basis to help her trust him again.

During their time in counseling, there were still concurrent stressors: B.'s medical issue, surgery for their twins (tonsils and adenoids removal), and demanding work schedules. L. is a nurse who works three 12-hour shifts per week, and B. is a teacher.

Upon completion of their counseling sessions, L. reported that she was moving forward and feeling better each day. B. agreed to have a few individual sessions to resolve his unfinished issues. L. made a choice from the beginning: she wanted her marriage to survive; everything she did followed that decision.

Two years later, when I called to get permission to use their story, it was not surprising to hear that everything was great. B. and L. thanked me for my help and agreed to let me use their story to help others. But, it wasn't me who made the difference. Because of their commitment to their marriage, they did what was needed to restore trust and faith in each other. They decided not to let an affair destroy their marriage. Instead they put a boundary around their relationship, prioritizing their union as a couple.

This is a letter I received from B.:

Dear Barbara:

*Here is how L. and I think that your counseling sessions helped us
. . .*

*Counseling helped me to realize the importance of communication.
In order to have a successful relationship/marriage, both of us
needed to be able to communicate effectively our thoughts and
our problems with one another (when we had problems). When
we started our sessions, I always felt that I loved L.; and despite
straying from our marriage, the sessions helped me to focus on that
love and why I wanted to make everything work.*

*Through our sessions, I realized how stupid it was to go outside our
marriage simply because I couldn't communicate (and chose not to
communicate with L.). Being able to express my feelings of regret,
remorse, shame, embarrassment, and disappointment in myself
during our sessions helped me to move on. I started on the road to
forgiving myself, although it was and still is at times a struggle for
me to do so. I have done it, however, for the most part.*

*Through our sessions, L. felt that she got help to hear from somebody
else that it was okay to forgive me. It was good to hear that it was
okay to try to make our marriage work, because the immediate
reaction was to end the marriage. Also, we both learned how to
build up our trust with one another again. Furthermore, L. feels
that through the sessions, like myself, in order to have a healthy
marriage, we learned the importance of communication, and the
importance of taking time for each other, not just our children and
our jobs.*
Over two years later, and we are doing GREAT right now!"

If this situation sounds familiar and you have experienced infidelity,
it is beneficial to know the roadblocks of looking back. Invariably
keeping the past as a reminder can only serve as a destructive force to
any future rebuilding. Couples who recover from affairs commit not to
let hurt or anger dominate. They voluntarily give up the right to keep

punishing, and decide to accept living with someone who has hurt them. They inevitably decide the good outweighs the bad, and they are able to have a realistic view of each partner's negatives and positives. Together they choose to move forward into a new and improved relationship.

Trust is the most important thing we can bestow upon a person. It is a risk; and we can leave ourselves open for loss. Our spouse is the one we trust most in the world. We trust them with our credit cards, our checkbooks, our children, and there may even come a time that we may have to trust them with our life.

When we put that much faith and trust into a person, we feel that they will always do what is best for us and put our needs ahead of their own. That is why betrayal hurts so much, and why it is so hard to forgive. If a husband or wife does something to break that trust, it often is a long road back to trusting again.

We might compare trust to a credit card. Suppose you are issued a card with a $10,000 credit limit. If you keep using the card, only making the minimum payments or no payments, the card quickly reaches its limit. If a person gives you his/her complete trust and you keep doing things to break that trust, you eventually overextend your credibility limit. Just as it will take a long time to dig out of the credit card debt, it will also take a long time to gain the other person's trust again. Sometimes it is not even possible to regain trust. But, if rebuilding is needed, there are some important points to remember.

First, be sure to communicate accurately, saying what you mean and asking for what you want. Second, make sure your actions match your words. Don't make a commitment to something you cannot deliver. It is best to commit to only what you will actively work on. What may seem harmless to the offender may seem like a betrayal to the other. Infidelity is often the most intense form of betrayal a couple can endure. It causes emotional pain, anger, fear, guilt, and shame, and it undermines the very foundation the marriage was built on in the beginning. When an affair is first discovered, the injured partner feels as if his/her world has collapsed. The injured party wonders if the marriage will remain intact or if it will end in divorce.

The good news is that it does not have to be the death of the relationship.

Some Extra Thought: Trust and Finances

Do you trust your spouse with your finances? Finances are sometimes the cause of problems, and sometimes a husband feels he can trust his wife with his heart, but not his checkbook.

Today it is so easy for couples to take on more debt than they can afford. Some couples get a mortgage that is too steep, and they could lose everything if they lost their jobs. A popular saying during the Great Depression was, "When poverty comes in the door, love goes out the window." This may not be true in every case, but finances can cause problems and may cause a lack of trust between marriage partners. Try to maintain trust by keeping your finances intact.

Some ways you can do this are:

Make a budget

Sit down together and plan how much money each of you requires for individual needs and household needs, and include those in your budget. Then, try to live within your budget.

Avoid buying on credit cards

Sometimes in emergencies, it can't be helped, but remember: emergencies do happen and credit cards should be available for them and used judiciously.

Strive for debt reduction

Try to pay extra on your mortgage, and try to save by watching for sales or having garage sales to reduce debt.

Save

Try to put something in a savings account each month, and save by recycling and being thrifty.

Try not to feel anxious

It may be hard for young couples to make ends meet, but anxiety drains emotional energy, causes people to make poor decisions, and causes couples to turn on each other with blame and accusations. Try to join together and work as a team in dealing with problems. Seek financial guidance when necessary.

"Those who live according to the sinful nature have their minds set upon what that nature desires: but those who live in accordance to the spirit have their minds set on what the spirit desires."

~ Romans 8:5

Chapter Nine

S Is for Spirituality

Hugh and Gayle Prather were an unlikely couple to develop a spiritual relationship. In his book *The Little Book of Letting Go*, Hugh relates the story from the beginning of their relationship. Just before his third date with Gayle, his two roommates asked if he was getting serious about her. He felt appalled by their question, explaining that they hardly knew each other. "We had spent only a total of eight hours together!" he writes. He pointed out that she had "the wrong politics, the wrong religion, and she smoked, drank and ate junk food. She had even been seen riding a motorcycle!"

Some time later, and much to his own surprise, as they sat in a coffeehouse, he asked, "Would you like to do something else?"

She answered, "Well, I guess so."

He then asked, "Would you like to get married?"

"Well, I guess so," she answered.

Since they lived in Dallas, Texas, where couples had to wait three days to get married, they drove toward Oklahoma where couples could get married immediately.

On the way, Gayle asked, "Do you think this is going to work out?"

"No," Hugh answered. "Do *you* think it's going to work out?"

"No," she said.

These two impulsive young people continued to Oklahoma, anyway, where they got married. Unbelievably, 45 years later, they are still happily married. Along the way, both became ministers. They have three sons, and they have authored many books together on the power of staying together as a couple.

So, how did they make it for 45 years? Each had a spiritual foundation that led to a desire to pursue individual and spiritual growth. That led to a firm foundation for developing their careers and maintaining a healthy marriage. Hugh calls Gayle his spiritual partner.

When couples have a spiritual base in their marriage, their marriage is more likely to succeed. Married couples can be happy for a short time, but for lasting contentment, it is important to develop a spiritual life.

Many of my clients in couples counseling have disclosed their faith or lack of any spiritual values. Occasionally, this very issue was the source of their conflict. But I have found that - when some component of faith was practiced - the marriage was stronger and the future more certain. It became one of the essential five qualities in order to have the gift of a lifetime.

Even when we work every day to improve ourselves and our marriages, sometimes we feel that something is lacking. There comes a time in every life when we must realize we must let go and let a higher power take over. We must live one day at a time and trust what we cannot see. This is spirituality. A quest or a spiritual journey is a very personal thing and can be very beautiful when shared with your mate.

Spirituality does not have to pertain to a specific religion or any organized religion, for that matter. Spirituality means that each person must develop according to his or her soul. Alcoholics Anonymous describes it as the "god of your own understanding." In other words, there is not "just one way" to pray, no exact method to meditate, and no required way to experience God.

Spirituality is an individual matter. We each need to experience spirituality from our own hearts, in our own unique approach. There is nothing inappropriate about creating a personal spiritual path. We each have an obligation to our souls to understand spirit from our heart's view. Accepting another's belief of how to fathom spirit is giving up a privilege that belongs only to our souls. I encourage you to "find your own way" and empower yourself with this freedom. The sooner we establish our own spirituality, the sooner we have peace . . . consequently, world peace.

Loving is one function of a spiritual life. As we advance spiritually, we exercise our capacity to serve others and to practice spirituality in our marriages. A spiritual couple is faithful. Fewer people are making life-long commitments, and sometimes, when they do take vows, they still break them. Sharing a belief in an eternal reality, or at least a practice, like prayer, of acknowledging the divine, makes staying committed a more realistic goal.

Being faithful in a relationship entails a solemn promise to God and one's spouse. This commitment should not be taken lightly or maintained only when we feel like it. We need to understand that our feelings can mislead us. Partners need to be faithful all of the time, not only whenever it is convenient for them. Similarly, people who desire good marriages do not look for people who will stay committed to them *most* of the time.

Remaining faithful to one's commitment is a character issue. A good marriage stands on long-term, trustworthy commitments - even under trying circumstances.

"Letting go" is a spiritual activity. When one partner pounds the other, trying to make the other change, the opposite usually happens. The gap between them widens. Turning the matter over to God can release the tension in the situation and can open the door to the couple working on the marriage.

Here is an activity that you can practice in order to pursue spiritual happiness. Suppose you and your mate have a problem, or you have something serious you need to discuss. Before approaching your partner, envision that your partner is going to be understanding. Envision being enlightened by a solution to the problem while the two of you are talking. Envision hugging each other at the end of the conversation. If you keep envisioning this as you approach discussing the problem, it can help.

Joel Osteen says, "God doesn't want you to drag through life defeated and depressed. God wants to restore your broken dreams. Maybe you were once excited about that person God brought into your life as a marriage partner, but now the excitement has worn off. Don't let that miracle slip away. Don't get so familiar with one another that you take each other for granted." Osteen talks about the first year that he and his wife, Victoria, dated. They laughed and had fun; they didn't have to do anything extravagant to be happy; they were in love, so they were happy just doing ordinary things.

You probably felt the same way with your partner, but now you get up in the morning and think, "That is just my wife or my husband," and you take it for granted that they will be there when you get home.

Osteen tells us that we need to take that few minutes to let each other know – you are appreciated. Rekindle the fire. God doesn't want you to simply survive in your marriage. He wants to turn it around and restore it to a strong, rewarding relationship. Enlarge your vision; develop a healthy self image, and discover the power of your thoughts and words. Osteen writes: "Let go of the past, stand strong against opposition and adversity, learn to give, and choose to be happy, God will take you places you've never dreamed of, and you will be living your best life now."

The movie *Fireproof* focuses on adult relationship issues surrounding a troubled marriage. The main character, a firefighter, whose motto is, "Never leave your partner behind," is a true hero in his work. At home, where he lives by his own rules, he is just another imperfect person unable to have a successful marriage. His wife, who always dreamed of marrying a loving brave firefighter, like her dad, wonders how she stopped being "good enough" for her husband.

The couple has regular arguments over jobs, finances, housework, and outside interests that move them to an indifferent, detached relationship. Facing a potential divorce, the firefighter submits to a 40-day challenge encouraged by his father and focused on faith based commitment. The firefighter begins putting *The Love Dare*, a book promoted by the movie, to use in solving his marital and personal challenges.

Eventually he sees his self-centeredness as a parasite contributing to a destructive force operating against his giving love freely. He perseveres in the hard work of reassembling his marriage, and at the end embraces the spirituality necessary to his success.

The Love Dare, written by Stephen and Alex Kendrick, offers this explanation of the connection between spirituality and marriage:

> *The Scriptures say that God designed and created marriage as a good thing. It is a beautiful, priceless gift. He uses marriage to help us eliminate loneliness, multiply our effectiveness, establish families, raise children, enjoy life and bless us with relational intimacy. But beyond this, marriage also shows us our need to grow and deal with our own issues and self-centeredness through the help of a lifelong partner. If we are teachable, we will learn*

to do the one thing that is most important in marriage—to love. His powerful union provides the path for you to learn how to love another imperfect person unconditionally. It is wonderful. It is difficult. It is life changing.

Fireproof shows a couple on the brink of divorce, who, through a commitment to love God, begin to reclaim their love for each other. It shows that, in order to love one another, you need the love of God first. When a relationship is right with God, then all others fall into place. It also shows the effect of self-indulgence and loving other things as a threat to the sacred covenant of marriage. The lesson learned here is to listen to one's heart, continue to learn about each other, and forgive.

According to David C. Olsen's book *The Spiritual Work of Marriage*, all human beings have a powerful need to be understood. This would be especially true between two people who are married to each other. "It is the experience of feeling like someone you care about really gets it." Feeling understood and accepted compliments the spiritual work of marriage.

"The spiritual work of marriage begins with recognizing the futility of trying to change one's partner," Olsen writes. "(It) . . . involves moving away from these destructive attempts to change one's partner and toward offering acceptance and grace."

He calls on individuals to look at what they contribute to the marriage, instead of "blaming the other and projecting onto the other one's own characteristics, which are the opposite of acceptance and grace," he points out.

"Most people are convinced that their relational problems are the fault of their partner, and they have difficulty seeing their own role in either the creation or maintaining of problems," Olsen says. "As a result, they continue the process of projection, and miss the opportunity for increased self-awareness." Olsen concludes, "A spiritual life is a life lived in relationship."

Some Extra Thought: Fireproofing Your Marriage

Make yourselves number one.

You are important to each other and therefore your needs take a front row seat. When your needs are met as a couple, then all else falls into place. Other's needs get met.

It is not selfish to take time for each other and strive to cherish and comfort one another.

That's what you agreed to in your vow to be together for the rest your lives.

Think of a bubble around your relationship.

Secure each other and make a safety net against all parasites that could detract from your focus on each other. Do not fall prey to outside influences that strive to manipulate your commitment to each other. Do not get tempted.

Words can heal wounds.

Rely on statements that buoy your partner. Praise your spouse's accomplishments purposely. Apologize when you have offended your partner. Words are important, because they communicate feelings that your spouse cannot see.

Share in a spiritual dialog.

A couple need not have exactly the same religious beliefs or view God the same way, but discussing these beliefs is an important indicator of the closeness of your relationship. Take time to describe how you view yourself as a spiritual person and listen to your spouse's description. When difficulty challenges your relationship, being able to interpret your partner's needs, based on a spiritual understanding, can be critical.

"I will no longer assume that my love partner can read my mind."

~ Larry James

Chapter Ten

Communication Is the Glue

The role of communication is a <u>must</u> in a book on marriage. It stands alone and really is evident in all of the FACTS; without meaningful communication, none of the FACTS could be practiced effectively.

Good communication between husband and wife is the glue that holds a marriage together, and it can be the difference between a happy relationship with someone, or one of contention and strife. It really is about getting to know each other with respect *for the other's* likes and dislikes. It is about respecting your spouse. I find it sad that there is not adequate preparation for communication during the courtship period. We all could use Communication 101.

Considering all the couples who have come to me for counseling, I can say with certainty that all of them needed better communication skills. What I have learned from my couples is that there are many reasons for their lack of communication skills - too lengthy to list. Most go back to their families and how they were taught; others are based on fears of confrontation; and some are just riddled with laziness. But what has been most obvious is the fact that people don't know how to talk to one another or to listen to their partner's needs.

Since communication was cited as a problem in most cases, it is necessary to address communication in every situation. One of the biggest hurdles for some clients is the difference in their own definitions for things. How something is defined is how it is acted upon, so if both people had different concepts of the same topic, the results would be confusion.

I often ask for clients' definitions of important concepts – time spent together, connection, listening, etc. It is amazing to hear the feedback. They are indeed surprised that they weren't even talking about the same subject; it opens up an awareness of the need to define appropriately what they were arguing about.

Earlier in the book, I referred to the technique of mirroring that helps clear up situations where definitions are misrepresented. Other areas of conflict came from the assumption area, when one client just simply perceived intention of the other, in essence making up their own interpretation without getting accurate information. Now the other person feels his spouse didn't listen to him/her and becomes defensive, thus beginning a negative feedback loop where neither feels satisfied.

I so often hear, "We just don't have anything to talk about anymore. I'm afraid if we go out on a date we will be sitting there without talking." Too often, couples get to this point. The question is, "why?"

Here are some responses I've heard:

1. We have grown apart.
2. All we have to talk about are the kids.
3. We are so tired at the end of the day; we just don't want to make conversation.

You can always find something to talk about with your spouse. The time you are together is special; talk about your dreams, goals, and your love for each other. The reason people get caught up in this dilemma is because they give up trying. I occasionally lose a couple in the counseling process when they hear I give homework, and I expect them to work on their marriage outside of the sessions. I always begin by setting the expectation that - if they want results - work must be done outside of my office. My homework assignments are designed to bring couples closer and to target the very issue causing them to separate.

One of the homework assignments I give is an exercise called "The Love Map," created by John Gottman. It consists of 60 questions for each to answer on how well they know their spouse. I often tell them to use it on date night and have fun with it. Many times it shows them how much or how little they actually know about each other. It definitely opens up communication venues that they didn't know existed. The couples I lose may go on to find other counselors and look for what they want to hear, but no matter whom they find, it will mean some sort of work.

Perhaps the word "work" needs to be defined in such a way that it depicts the true nature of marriage. Happiness and fulfillment do not come automatically because a vow is taken.

In addition to the ideas presented above, the essential components of effective communication are:

Listening attentively to one another;
Clearly stating the point, without filters;
Choosing an appropriate response for the content;
Delivering the response in a loving, but direct manner;
Being open to re-negotiation if necessary.

When I worked as a nurse, we always had to make sure our nursing care plan had a section called "modification of plan." This is what I refer to in the last component: being able to take another approach if the first one failed to achieve the desired results.

There is another skill I teach my clients to use called the "criticism sandwich." The first sentence (the first slice of bread) is a positive statement; the second one (the filling) is the criticism or complaint; and the third (second piece of bread) is a positive statement. You are surrounding the criticism or complaint with two positive layers because people usually hear the first and last sentence better.

Here's an example. "Honey, I love the way you help with the children in the morning when things are hectic, and we are trying to get everyone out of the house for work and school. However, I wish you could check their rooms before they leave to insure that their beds are made and their clothes are put away. I come home from work, and I get so irritated when I see their rooms so messy. But, I don't know what I would do without your help each day. You are a great husband."

Communication can also use the other senses. Often couples communicate with body language. When your husband walks through the door in the evening after a long day at work, can't you tell by his gait and the expression on his face what type of mood he is in, or if something bad has happened at work?

Do you know that little secret smile you exchange at a cocktail party when you know the person talking is exaggerating? How about that little hand squeeze under the table at a company dinner that says you are both bored and would rather be eating at McDonald's?

Body language is often your clue to come to the other person's rescue, and comfort them or share in their joy. Body language is effective communication.

Sometimes when a couple has been married for a long time, they can sit together on the porch gazing at a sunset, without speaking, each lost in their own thoughts or memories. This type of silence can be communication. Often, after sitting like this, when the couple does speak, they find they were thinking about the same thing or sharing a memory.

It is important to be able to be fallible and vulnerable with your spouse. No one can be right all the time, and it is okay to let your spouse know when you are miserable or hurting. Let your spouse see your weaknesses and let him/her help you. It is okay to let someone else be strong sometimes.

In his book, *Marriage is for Adults*, Dr. James R. McCormick says, "I believe strongly that there is no intimacy without vulnerability. Show me a person who is always strong, always self-sufficient, and always right, and I will show you a person we may admire, but one with whom we cannot be intimate. We can only get close to a person who is vulnerable, who needs something from us. The person who is never needy or vulnerable will always keep us at arm's length, and communication will be difficult. My guess is that arrogance, pride, stubbornness, dogmatism, and pettiness have ruined far more marriages than adultery ever did."

Some Extra Thought: In An Argument, Time is Not on Your Side

In the art of communication we can't ignore that healthy conflict often gets neglected.

Healthy conflict involves healthy communication. In everyday life, people often have disagreements, and the way they resolve those disagreements is often an indication of their command of communication skills.

Poor communication skills can have disastrous effects on a marriage as seen when conflict doesn't get resolved.

We all get angry, and we all argue with the people we love. Arguments can be beneficial. We need to hear another point of view, and we need to challenge ourselves to grow and see things from a different perspective. Resentment, however, is never healthy. When you argue with someone you care about, time is not on your side.

We expect a relationship to be a caring, cooperative, pleasing and loving union of two or more people. It can be a man and a woman, a family, a friendship or a work relationship. A central theme to its success lies in how anger gets communicated and whether or not it turns into the debilitating emotion of resentment. As defined, resentment means: "the feeling of displeasure or indignation at something regarded as an injury or insult."

Anger is a natural emotion. It could occur by being in a traffic jam on the interstate, getting frustrated at the kids because they are not getting up on time for school, or having a computer problem disrupting a work project. Whatever the cause, it rears its ugly head many times a day. The expression of anger is different from the feeling. Expressed appropriately, it is a necessary emotion; expressed inappropriately makes it unhealthy.

Healthy anger is purposeful and allows for you to face the cause, set boundaries for yourself and determine what you need to do in response. It is not used to punish, intimidate, control or manipulate the other person. It is expressed and discussed to resolve a situation. If it is stuffed down or ignored, it becomes resentment. This in turn can create physical, mental and emotional problems.

Never wait on talking to someone about a concern that bothers you. Time is not in your favor here, and acting quickly can save a situation from going sour. Pushing feelings down makes it impossible to work through conflict and tends to keep a person trapped. When discussing these issues, always make sure you understand the point of view and where that person is coming from. Ask questions. It may sound like this: "If I change my behavior regarding.......will you let go of your anger?"

Know your bottom line. Will you continue to act in your own best interest or fall prey to another's unrealistic and unattainable request? Will you continue to try and try despite the un-willingness of your spouse, co-worker, etc. to be accepting of your efforts?

Arguments can be beneficial. We need to hear another point of view, and we need to challenge ourselves to grow and see things from a different perspective. What we don't want to happen is to be pulling our weight when the other person is merely on the receiving end. Of course, a visit to a counselor can help intervene in relationship disputes and provide some workable ideas towards problem resolution.

"Faith is being sure of what we hope for and certain of what we do not see."

~ Hebrews 11:1

Chapter Eleven

FAITH Empowers the FACTS

The FACTS are a collection of behaviors and habits that successful married couples use to strengthen their relationship, and we can learn from their example. When a marriage is strong, certain visible indicators exist. We will use another acronym to discuss this: the word FAITH. I often ask couples to tell me what they see as the most important components of a successful marriage. The answers are varied, but most agree on the following five that I call FAITH. In addition to the FACTS, these five complement, and add the finishing touches, to the gift of a lifetime.

Our faith in God, in ourselves, and in our spouse will bring us to the fulfillment of a good marriage disciplined by faith. In the Greek language, "faith" also meant faithfulness. We should be faithful to God, to our spouse, and to ourselves.

The Fruit of FAITH explained.

F . . . is for friendship.

You have heard it said, "Always marry your best friend." A best friend is one you can count on in good and bad, one you can be yourself with, and one who does not judge or condemn your behavior. They accept you for who you are, and it's easy to talk to them, ask an opinion, and give advice. There are no false pretenses. "What you see is what you get," and there are no surprises later; no expectations or demands. They laugh with you, and cry with you; and they never abandon or disrespect you.

We choose our friends and give our time and effort to the friendship, for it, too, takes work to survive, but the rewards are worth all the effort. As a quality in a marriage, it can't be beat, and it is part of a strong foundation for being together for life. As love changes during the years, friendship remains constant.

All good marriages are built on faithfulness. A good friend is a faithful friend, and not just *some* of the time. Proverbs states, "A friend is one who loves at all times" (17:17).

A . . . is for affection.

Do you still hold hands in the movies? How about when you are taking a walk? These little signs of affection mean a lot. While it is not good to show an open display of untactful affection in public, a nice smile or wink for your partner across a crowded room shows them you care. If you pack a lunch for your husband, a simple love note will no doubt bring a smile to his lips. Send a text message that says, "I love you." Get reservations at your favorite restaurant for no special occasion, and surprise your wife with a night out; or bring a grocery store bouquet of flowers home with you from work. These acts of affection help ease bumps in the road.

I have talked with many people who have become widowed, and it is the affection from a spouse that they miss the most. Sometimes we refer to it as the "little things," but we all know that little things can mean a lot.

One widow said she missed sitting on the lawn with her husband on a summer night watching the stars. She thinks now her late husband is one of those stars and is watching over her. Another widow misses her husband bringing her coffee and the newspaper each morning. Yet another widow misses her husband picking a bouquet of flowers for her from their yard. One widower misses his wife always placing clean handkerchiefs on his bureau where he could find them, and baking a chocolate cake for him every month. The list goes on, but it is always the small affectionate things that leave a lasting spot in one's memory.

Do you remember how special it made you feel to receive flowers or a gift for no special occasion, just because someone thought you were special?

I . . . is for intimacy.

Family therapist and author, Richard C. Schwartz, describes intimacy in this very powerful way: "Intimacy is often defined as the ability to reveal all aspects of oneself to another and feel accepted.

Because you aren't ashamed or afraid of your vulnerable parts, you can expose them to your partner and experience the joy of being fully known and witnessed by another." Many of us have learned that being vulnerable is not pleasing to others and we have learned to hide these emotions.

In a true intimate relationship, your spouse can be supportive and compassionate to those feelings and provide acceptance for your having them. You will be able to share your secrets and innermost thoughts without fearing rejection, making it easier for your spouse to know you thoroughly and love you fully.

Another aspect of intimacy has often been compared to sexual activity. Although that is a part of it, intimacy can mean other things such as a backrub from a partner after a tiring day at work or a foot massage. It can mean cuddling on the couch while watching television, or a romantic candlelight dinner for two. Intimacy can just be talking about a problem or the day's events. Intimacy means something that just the two of you share that brings you closer together as a couple.

Before the so-called "sexual revolution" of the 1960's, it was believed that the ideal sexual situation was a bond between a husband and a wife. The sexual revolution was supposed to free everyone to explore sex outside of marriage. It freed men and women to separate sex from commitment. But the sexual revolution wasn't so free after all, because decades later we are reaping its consequences. Forty-five million people in the United States have a sexually transmitted disease. The biggest cause of poverty in the United States is single women trying to raise children, because they did not marry the father of their children or don't even know who the father is. The only real safe sex is between a husband and a wife who have been faithful to each other.

Men and women differ significantly in their feelings regarding sex. Men are capable of having sex without much encouragement; women need encouragement and romance. It is vital that the communication loop is open so they can tell each other their wants, needs, and fantasies. "Women often give sex to get intimacy, and men give intimacy to get sex," said Dr. James Dobson in his book, *Love for a Lifetime*.

As women are, by nature, usually more romantically inclined, the man who pays attention to her with small acts of affection during the day will ultimately create a more satisfying sexual relationship for both.

"To make the most of the physical dimension of marriage, a man must pursue his wife's mind as well as her body," Dr. Dobson added.

I often hear discrepancies in this area from my couples. It is usually the wife who has given up on the sexual/intimate aspect of the relationship. This of course creates conflict for the male. Many of the women say they are fine with the way things are. They are busy with their kids, careers, friends, etc., and appear to be fulfilled. Some even say that at the end of the day, it is only another "chore."

There are many books written on the subject of sex, and most of the leading women's magazines have sections devoted to it every month. Television shows and movies all attempt to have a sexual component. Sex is a "hot" topic (no pun intended), and it does need its place within a satisfying marriage.

Tenderness, affection, and trust play important roles in your sex life. Always make the other person's needs as important as your own. Never initiate sex when your partner is not feeling well, and remember to use endearing words like darling, sweetheart, or baby. Words are important, especially the words "I love you."

In sex and in all marital relationships, it is always important to remember: Love is not supposed to hurt.

God gave marriage, and the sexual union within marriage, as a gift to you. God didn't create sex just to produce children. It is meant to be the best way to show affection between a husband and a wife.

T . . . is for time.

"Yet the timeless in you is aware of life's timelessness, and knows that yesterday is but today's memory and tomorrow is today's dream." (*The Prophet*, Kahlil Gibran)

The most valuable thing we have is our time. I'm sure you go to bed many nights feeling that there are not enough hours in the day for you to accomplish all that you need to accomplish.

Employers say "time is money," and that is true. So, if we give people a few hours of our time, we are giving them a gift.

Could you miss one Sunday afternoon ball game to have a date with your wife? Could you get a sitter for one evening in order to have an evening alone with your husband? What about dinner at the dining room table instead of in front of the television? Do you really take time to listen to your partner and see what he/she is going through?

There are always going to be activities that demand our time, but instead of always being in a hurry, try to "stop and smell the roses." If more time was spent in communicating and enjoying life together, many problems could be avoided.

I often share the following story with my clients:

What if someone gave you $1,440 every day and deposited it into your account but told you there was one criterion that needed to be met: you had to spend it all or you would not receive the $1,440 the next day. What would you do?

You do have such a bank account; only it is not money. It is time. Every day you have 1,440 minutes given to you. How you choose to spend those 1,440 minutes is up to you. If you do not spend them in a positive way, they are gone. You cannot decide that you want to repeat them; so wouldn't it be prudent to use them with the very best intentions? That way you would never have regrets and your bank account would remain full. So, time spent with our spouse is another gift we give to them.

Talents are another gift we possess. Each of us should use all of our talents to make our life and our marriage successful. Could you serenade your wife with a song, if you have the gift of a beautiful voice? Could you write her a sweet love song if you are a writer? Could you knit your husband a sweater or bake him a delicious dinner? All of our special talents come to play most in our marriages and are also a way to make our time well used and enjoyable.

H . . . is for happiness.

All of us seek happiness. But, happiness doesn't come just from the "highs" in life but the joy of doing everyday things. You may be preparing for marriage or are about to have a new baby, or you might be in a desperate situation, or on the brink of divorce, but part of your happiness will be embracing today and taking on the challenge of change. We need to enjoy every minute of our lives.

All of us seek happiness. Most of us have been acculturated with the idea that someone makes you happy. We now know that is not so.

Actually happiness is an inside job. It resides in you; it is an emotion that we choose to give ourselves.

Let me illustrate through Victor Frankel's description of the prisoners in his book, *Man's Search for Meaning*. According to a 1991 survey conducted by Book-of-the-Month Club and the Library of Congress, Frankel's book made a list of the 10 most influential books in the United States. In the book, Frankel reports his experiences as a concentration camp inmate. His account of life as a prisoner in concentration camps serves as an example of the ability of the human being to freely choose his or her attitude. He describes the prisoners in the concentration camps waiting for their moment of death. He said that the prisoners were stripped of all belongings along with removal of body hair. What remained were bare bodies, or as Frankel describes it, naked existence. However, there was one thing no one could take away from them: it was their attitude and the way they wished to see the world. If they wanted to look out of their small cell window and see a sunset or sunrise and feel some joy in what they saw, they could.

Frankel concluded that the meaning of life is found in every moment of living, even in the face of death. You might find this hard to understand and question why these prisoners would make that choice in the face of their impending demise. I suppose the answer is quite simple. It was their choice to feel happy, even for a fleeting moment. Everyone has the choice to decide to be happy or sad. It is not dependent on anyone else. No one owes us; no one is responsible for us. We are the author of our lives. In this role we can certainly make many choices. We get to choose our every thought and action, much like the playwright, creating the script for the actors to follow. What an opportunity!

Some Extra Thought: A Happy State of Mind

1. Reduce your stress level. Your occupation may be stressful, but try to obtain balance by getting enough sleep and exercise. Exercise is one of the best ways to reduce stress.

2. Eat a proper diet and get fresh air. Try to spend some time outside each day. Sun is healing and often brings happiness. Also noticing the beauty in nature, such as birds, flowers and rainbows contributes to happiness. Diet is very important. Eat balanced meals, and get proper food from each of the food groups every day.

3. Meet with other people. You and your spouse may be happy being alone, but association with other couples that have your common interests is healthy and builds community.

4. Have fun. Do you enjoy movies, plays, theme parks or shopping? Then engage in these things with your spouse. Sharing fun things that will have you laughing leads to happiness.

5. Develop spirituality. As you study the meaning of life and the existence of a Higher Power, then you realize that you do not have to face life's responsibilities alone. People were designed for a connection with God, and an enlightened spiritual journey aids in achieving happiness.

6. Live in the moment. No one can survive on memories alone. Yesterday's memories may be wonderful or sad, but they are still a part of yesterday. Today is a new day; leave your memories, and move on with your life. Don't always think that you will do something tomorrow. Plan and prepare for tomorrow, but enjoy life today.

*"You must love yourself before you love another.
By accepting yourself and fully being what you are . . .
your simple presence can make others happy."*

~ Jane Roberts

Chapter Twelve

What's Love Got to Do with It?

Tina Turner asks in her famous song, "What's love got to do with it?" In marriage, love has just about everything to do with it.

In working with clients, one thing I hear almost every day is: "I love my husband very much, but I am no longer in love with him." When I question them further, I hear that the romance, attention, and sexual attraction they had in the beginning of their relationship has faded. There is little effort on either part to keep the fire burning. They became strangers with respect for each other, allowing other things to fill the void, such as a job, or the kids, or an addiction - anything but each other.

The first thing these couples need to learn is that as marriage evolves and goes through changes, so do the way partners feel about each other. The romantic, sexual love we felt in the beginning will develop into something deeper and more meaningful, but often we still wish for that thrill of beginning love. So we must search for ways to keep that spark alive and have that thrill, along with the advantages of a deeper relationship.

Let's begin by looking at the meaning of love and the many faces of love. Agape is a Greek word for love representing the type of love God has for us. As a verb, it depicts the type of love God wants people to have for one another. God's love is spiritual and not emotional. Reflecting the fact that human marriage is modeled after the divine relationship between Christ and his church, husbands are told to love their wives with this kind of love; which is outgoing and does not think about itself (Ephesians 5:25, 31-32). True love isn't focused on oneself or one's feelings or emotions but in outward love toward others. It is best described in Corinthians, "Love is patient; love is kind; it does not envy; it does not boast; it is not proud; it is not rude; it isn't self seeking; it is slow to anger; it keeps no record of wrongs; love does not delight in evil but rejoices in truth." It protects, trusts, hopes and preserves; but best of all it tells us that love never fails.

Eros refers to exotic love or desire. It pertains to a large physical attraction between two people that is often based on chemistry. This is the type of love that makes you want to be with the other person constantly. This love is what many creative arts are built upon, and countless books, plays and movies use this as their central theme. This is the type of love that usually attracts us to our mate, and it is the type of love that causes us to copulate and produce children. So, it is important in a relationship.

Since the lust and attraction stages are both temporary, a third stage is needed to have a long-term relationship. Attachment is the bonding factor that usually leads to marriage and children.

Psychology depicts love as a co-genitive and social phenomenon. It is based on intimacy, commitment, and passion. Andrew Newberg, a neuroscientist, suggests that love affects the same area of the brain as drugs. Scientists believe love is an activity and not just a feeling.

Romance is a general term that refers to a celebration of life through art, music, and the attempt to express love with deeds. Romance can be defined as attachment, fascination, or enthusiasm for something or someone. Most psychological research suggests that romantic love lasts for about a year and then dies or is replaced by a more enduring form of love known as companionate love. In companionate love, basic friendship and trust are essential, but romantic feelings diminish. However, new research suggests that couples could and should keep romantic feelings alive. Romantic love is usually the first step toward a lifelong commitment.

People can make the first step toward a lifelong commitment with this type of love, but to have a more enduring type of love, other things must follow. Before one can truly love another person, she/he must love and respect themselves.

Many people have unhappy childhoods in which they did not receive proper nurturing and love; therefore, it is hard for them to love themselves. Sometimes it takes individual counseling to work through this "sludge pile" before a person from that background can commit to a relationship. Once one holds oneself in high regard and is doing things to make one's own life better, she/he can then focus on another person. Taking care of physical, emotional, and spiritual needs should be a priority; once you are on good terms with yourself, you are ready to enter a relationship.

Opposites usually attract, and this is good because in that way the two can enhance each other; but usually it is the similarities between two that bind them together.

Although romantic love is needed to attract one to another person, it is an immature type of love. In a relationship that is long lasting, we must strive for a more mature type of love. This is a deep and spiritual connection between two individuals that is not based on sex alone. In platonic love, one person inspires the other and directs the other toward spiritual matters. Some only have a platonic type of love in their relationship. This often happens between older couples, but if we can combine romantic and platonic love, they will lead us to a path of more spiritual love.

Even in a relationship, we must remain individuals, true to ourselves and our own needs. We must operate as two individual identities that come together and complement each other and create a dynamic and spiritual relationship that stands the test of time.

Erich Fromm said: "Immature love says, 'I love you because I need you.' Mature love says, 'I need you because I love you.'"

In her book *The Truth About Love*, Dr. Pat Love writes, "The Eastern approach defines love as the desire to make someone happy. But the Western approach says, 'What can you do to make me happy?'" In other words, if you treat me like I want to be treated, then I will be happy, and I will love you. One theory is not any more empirically true, but love is, in part, about getting your needs met. The only thing it shows is that using your talents for a worthy cause can make us happy. We are all absorbed with our reality, and we think our partner should see everything as we do. This is not true. Sometimes when a marriage gets into trouble, a man and woman realize that they are reading from a different script.

Change is what keeps us afloat. As we grow older, and if we refuse to change, we become outdated and stuck in a rut. We must be willing to change. Like a little rubber duck that sits on the beach and is washed in and out with the tide, we must learn to go with the flow and not to try to swim upstream or run into the wind, but have the winds to our backs. This way, if we accept change and learn to grow and mature with the years, then we will accept the changes in our relationship.

"Grow old along with me . . . the best is yet to be." This quotation from Elizabeth Browning says it best. As the years pass, and we practice the FACTS that hold together a marriage, we will see our love mature. No one says it will be easy. We must sacrifice a lot along the way, but each sacrifice brings its own reward.

We all require variety and freshness in our life to stay alert and active, so search for ways to keep your marriage alive and active. Enjoy doing things together; keep the lines of communication open; and remember the romantic love that attracted you in the first place. Practice the FACTS empowered by FAITH. Embrace tomorrow, but love as if this was your last day on earth.

The movie *The Bucket List* gives us a picture of love at the core. In this funny and heart warming movie, two hospital roommates with terminal illnesses become friends. One is a billionaire, the other a scholarly mechanic. They decide to compose a list of all the things they want to do before they die. This sends them to the "around the world" adventure of their lives: sky diving, race car driving, seeing the Great Pyramid of Khufu, and more. Somewhere along the way, the scholarly mechanic gets homesick and decides to abandon the last part of the adventure to go home to spend his last days with his wife. He finds out that his love for her and their marriage was the only thing that should have been on his list, all the while right in front of him on a daily basis. He went home and loved her as if it was his last day alive.

Looking at a picture of your loved one always brings thoughts. It has been said a picture is worth a thousand words, and though it might not produce a thousand words, you might be surprised by the conversation that takes place.

Pick a photo that leads to discussion and ask your partner what thoughts or memories it brings to mind. Give the other person time to think, look and offer thoughts. Probe further: "What in the picture makes you say that?" There is never any right or wrong answer. This time is designed to be fun for both of you. It is a time to cherish.

I am a romantic at heart, and I feel love letters are something that men and women both cherish. Remember in the marriage vow when you promised to cherish your spouse? Cherish means to hold them in high regard and affection, and a love letter is proof of this affection. In *The Bridges of Madison County* by Robert James Waller, there is an example of a wonderful love letter. The last paragraph reads: "But, I am, after all, a man. And all the philosophic rationalizations I can conjure up do not keep me from wanting you, every day, every moment, the merciless wail of time, of time I can never spend with you, deep within my head. I love you, profoundly and completely, and I always will."

Some Extra Thought: Love Letters

The following story by Arnold Fine, first published by The Jewish Press, captures beautifully the power of a letter between lovers.

As I walked home one freezing day, I stumbled on a wallet someone had lost in the street. I picked it up and looked inside to find some identification so I could call the owner. But the wallet contained only three dollars and a crumpled letter that looked as if it had been in there for years.

The envelope was worn, and the only thing that was legible on it was the return address. I started to open the letter, hoping to find some clue. The letter had been written almost sixty years ago. It was written in a beautiful feminine handwriting, on powder blue stationery with a little flower in the left-hand corner. It was a "Dear John" letter that told the recipient, whose name appeared to be Michael, that the writer could not see him anymore, because her mother forbade it. Even so, she wrote that she would always love him. It was signed, Hannah.

It was a beautiful letter, but there was no way, except for the name Michael, that the owner could be identified. Maybe if I called information, the operator could find a phone listing for the address on the envelope.

"Operator," I began, "this is an unusual request. I'm trying to find the owner of a wallet that I found. Is there any way you can tell me if there is a phone number for an address that was on an envelope in the wallet?"

She suggested I speak with her supervisor, who hesitated for a moment then said, "Well, there is a phone listing at that address, but I can't give you the number." She said, as a courtesy, she would call that number, explain my story and would ask them if they wanted her to connect me. I waited a few minutes and then she was back on the line. "I have a party who will speak with you."

I asked the woman on the other end of the line if she knew anyone by the name of Hannah. She gasped, "Oh! We bought this house from a family who had a daughter named Hannah. But that was 30 years ago!"

"Would you know where that family could be located now?" I asked.

"I remember that Hannah had to place her mother in a nursing home some years ago," the woman said. "Maybe if you got in touch with them they might be able to track down the daughter."

She gave me the name of the nursing home and I called the number. They told me the old lady had passed away some years ago but they did have a phone number for where they thought the daughter might be living.

I thanked them and phoned. The woman who answered explained that Hannah herself was now living in a nursing home. This whole thing was stupid, I thought to myself. Why was I making such a big deal over finding the owner of a wallet that had only three dollars and a letter that was almost sixty years old?

Nevertheless, I called the nursing home in which Hannah was supposed to be living, and the man who answered the phone told me, "Yes, Hannah is staying with us."

Even though it was already 10 p.m., I asked if I could come by to see her. "Well," he said hesitatingly, "if you want to take a chance, she might be in the day room watching television."

I thanked him and drove over to the nursing home. The night nurse and a guard greeted me at the door. We went up to the third floor of the large building. In the day room, the nurse introduced me to Hannah, a sweet, silver-haired old timer with a warm smile and a twinkle in her eye.

I told her about finding the wallet and showed her the letter. The second she saw the powder blue envelope with that little flower on the left, she took a deep breath and said, "Young man, this letter was the last contact I ever had with Michael."

She looked away for a moment, deep in thought, and then said softly, "I loved him very much. But I was young at the time and my mother felt I was too young. Oh, he was so handsome. He looked like Sean Connery, the actor."

"Yes," she continued. "Michael Goldstein was a wonderful person. If you should find him, tell him I think of him often. And . . ." she hesitated for a moment, almost biting her lip, "tell him I still love him. You know," she said smiling as tears began to well up in her eyes, "I never did marry. I guess no one ever matched up to Michael . . ."

I thanked Hannah and said good-bye. I took the elevator to the first floor and as I stood by the door, the guard there asked, "Was the old lady able to help you?"

I told him she had given me a lead. "At least I have a last name. But, I think I'll let it go for a while. I spent almost the whole day trying to find the owner of this wallet."

I had taken out the wallet, which was a simple brown leather case with red lacing on the side. When the guard saw it, he said, "Hey, wait a minute! That's Mr. Goldstein's wallet. I'd know it anywhere with that bright red lacing. He's always losing that wallet. I must have found it in the halls at least three times."

"Who's Mr. Goldstein?" I asked as my hand began to shake.

"He's one of the old timers on the 8th floor. That's Mike Goldstein's wallet for sure. He must have lost it on one of his walks."

I thanked the guard and quickly ran back to the nurse's office.

I told her what the guard had said. We went back to the elevator and got on. I prayed that Mr. Goldstein would be up.

On the eighth floor, the floor nurse said, "I think he's still in the day room. He likes to read at night. He's a darling old man."

We went to the only room that had any lights on and there was a man reading a book. The nurse went over to him and asked if he had lost his wallet. Mr. Goldstein looked up with surprise, put his hand in his back pocket and said, "Oh, it *is* missing!"

"This kind gentleman found a wallet and we wondered if it could be yours?"

I handed Mr. Goldstein the wallet and the second he saw it, he smiled with relief and said, "Yes, that's it! It must have dropped out of my pocket this afternoon. I want to give you a reward."

"No, thank you," I said. "But I have to tell you something. I read the letter in the hope of finding out who owned the wallet." The smile on his face suddenly disappeared. "You read that letter? "Not only did I read it, I think I know where Hannah is." He suddenly grew pale. "Hannah? You know where she is? How is she? Is she still as pretty as she was? Please, please tell me," he begged.

""She's fine...just as pretty as when you knew her." I said softly.

The old man smiled with anticipation and asked, "Could you tell me where she is? I want to call her tomorrow." He grabbed my hand and said, "You know something, mister, I was so in love with that girl that when that letter came, my life literally ended. I never married. I guess I've always loved her."

"Mr. Goldstein," I said, "Please come with me."

We took the elevator down to the third floor. The hallways were darkened and only one or two little night-lights lit our way to the day room where Hannah was sitting alone watching the television. The nurse walked over to her.

"Hannah," she said softly, pointing to Michael, who was waiting with me in the doorway. "Do you know this man?"

Hannah adjusted her glasses, looked for a moment, but didn't say a word. Michael said softly, almost in a whisper, "Hannah, it is Michael. Do you remember me?"

She gasped, "Michael! I don't believe it! Michael! It's you! My Michael!"

He walked slowly towards her and they embraced. The nurse and I left with tears streaming down our faces. "See," I said. "See how the Good Lord works! If it's meant to be, it will be."

About three weeks later I got a call at my office from the nursing home. "Can you break away on Sunday to attend a wedding? Michael and Hannah are going to tie the knot!"

It was a beautiful wedding with all the people at the nursing home dressed up to join in the celebration. Hannah wore a light beige dress and looked beautiful. Michael wore a dark blue suit and stood tall. They made me their best man.

The hospital gave them their own room and if you ever wanted to see a 76-year-old bride and a 79-year-old groom acting like two teenagers, you had to see this couple.

A perfect ending for a love affair that had lasted nearly 60 years. Many people will walk in and out of your life, but only love will leave footprints in your heart.

Now that you know the FACTS of happy couples, how do you rate your marriage? Sometimes these simple facts are more difficult to practice than just simply reading them and saying, "Yes, I'll do that!" It must be a daily reminder. I suggest you list these facts and cut them out and post them on your refrigerator door or over your bathroom mirror so that you will be reminded of them several times a day - or refer to them often if you are having problems. Put a list in your purse or in your car; keep them with you always.

Now it is your turn to share your innermost thoughts with the one with whom you have chosen to spend your life. Please use the next page to write a love letter to your spouse and present this book as your gift. Say as much or as little as you want, but say what you want him or her to remember forever. If you plan to keep this book or share it intimately with your spouse, write your letter on the next page. If you plan to present the book to someone else, use a separate sheet of paper.

Love Letter

_____

_____

_____

_____

_____

_____

_____

_____

_____

_____

_____

_____

_____

_____

_____

_____

_____

Love Letter

_____
_____
_____
_____
_____
_____
_____
_____
_____
_____
_____
_____
_____
_____
_____

"More family members also means more love, and that is a huge advantage for any child."

~ Darlene Zagata, "Advantages of a Blended Family"

A Last Whisper in Your Ear

The blended family cannot be overlooked. In an article written by Alesha Thomas, contributing writer for *Business Innovators Magazine*, she states, "According to the American Psychological Association, 40%–50% of all first marriages in the United States end in divorce. The rate of divorce in remarriages is even higher—at approximately 75%. Experts predict that this growing trend will result in the 'blended family' becoming the predominant family structure in the United States."

She goes on to say, "This type of family structure comes with a unique set of challenges that traditional marriage counseling and training may not address."

These figures tell the story: Second, third, and more marriages are part of life in this country. For this reason alone, blended families are increasing in number. The children from each past marriage go on to have a major impact on a new marriage. Whether the "children" are adults, teenagers, children, or much younger, they all cause challenges and add a new dimension to a marriage. If they will not accept their mom or dad's new spouse, it dramatically increases the odds that a new marriage may not survive. But today many marriages have children from more than one father and mother. The resulting family system is indeed complicated.

Here are some questions you might have overlooked before you said "I do":

- Did you talk about how you would deal with each other's children?
- Did you talk about how you would deal with the "ex's"?
- Did you talk about your own child-rearing styles and ways of discipline?
- Did you paint a picture of what it was like in your previous relationship with the children?
- Did you clearly state your ideas of how to interact with the former parent and indicate how much of a presence that person would have in the new blended family?

While the help in this book is exactly what you need, keep in mind these SOS basics.

Successful Outcome Steps

1. Understand that blending a family requires time and needs everyone's commitment to pursue the challenges effectively. It may take several months or years to reach the happy place of the new family. This is when patience becomes your best friend. In this case, expecting a short internship will probably lead to disappointment. Practice delayed gratification on this one. It could be worth it.

2. Prepare for relationship changes. If you had a positive relationship with the child of your partner before marriage, it can change once you tie the knot to become a stepparent. Discipline comes into place with young children and parenting styles get challenged. Power struggles surface. There may be significant differences in how each of you parented. There are new roles in the new family, and the boundaries need to be set.

3. Create a shared list of values with your blended family. Find things that are unique to the new family members. Make some family time to encourage new ideas. A family meeting is a great way to accomplish this task.

4. Build new household rules, unique to the new family structure. Get input from all family members. Compliance works best when there is shared input. Allow children to suggest some rules of their own.

5. Make schedules. Most families in today's world with school-age children run on schedules. In a blended family, your life will live by schedules because you've added more moving parts to the equation. Make certain that the schedules allow for these important things:

Time to all be together.

Time to be with just your kids.

Time to be with just their kids.

Time to be alone as a couple.

Taking two or three hours "off" as a couple to go out to dinner or go for a walk reinforces your marriage and status as a couple.

6. Deal with the ex. A healthy marriage can take place when you find a way of dealing with your spouse's ex. Manage your negative feelings about this person. Communicate with the ex consistently, and establish boundaries. Dealing with the ex shows your current spouse that you're truly there to support the new family and be part of the team. You're interested in *all* of your spouse's life. Set a rule not to speak negatively about your spouse's ex. Negative speaking sets a bad example for your kids and weakens your marriage. Try to find the good parts of your ex and focus on that. The kids' self-esteem is reinforced by positive statements but weakened by negative ones. Remember they came from the biological parents and will share 50% of each of them.

7. Incorporate some of the traditions from your previous individual family and make some new ones together. How are birthdays celebrated? Are good grades rewarded in special ways? Maintaining traditions respects and honors the lives you lived before you and your spouse got married. Adding new family traditions reinforces the stability of the new family.

There's something else I'd like to whisper in your ear:

Blended families are not a sociological problem. Instead, this type of family structure can offer certain advantages. Let's call it a "value-added family" and see how that changes your perspective.

What has been added to your blended family that is of value? Well, first of all, you are hopefully a lot happier and more optimistic in this new marriage. Having discovered, perhaps painfully, what doesn't work, you now have an opportunity to enjoy a much better "fit." When our adult needs for intimacy, affection, financial security, and trustworthiness are being met, we can't help but be better parents as well. Research has shown that even in marriages where an attempt is made to hide parental discord, children are aware of the fact that their parents are in a state of friction and unhappiness. Being children (of any age!), they will certainly test the limits and boundaries of a new situation, just to make sure the adults are doing their jobs as moms or dads. Your personal happiness models important information for all of the children. They can learn what a good marriage looks like by seeing how you and your new spouse treat one another. This increases their chances for successful, long-term partnerships when they are of an age to tackle that developmental phase.

If you look at a blended family as an opportunity to learn new ways to love other people and express your compassion, you have made a good beginning.

"Though no one can go back and make a brand new start, anyone can start now and make a brand new ending."

~ Carl Bard

Epilogue

The Gift that Keeps on Giving

It's now up to you to make your marriage last a lifetime. Most self-help books are read, discussed, and then put away, although many have good information and offer wonderful thoughts of adding quality to one's life. Why is it they are not used as manuals and acted upon?

When I recommend the book *Men are From Mars, Women are from Venus* to my clients, I often hear: "Oh, I think we have that book somewhere in our house;" or, "I read it a long time ago, and I don't know where it is now." This is a common response and implies that most of us only want to read a book and not have to take any action, because if it involves some sort of work, many lose interest.

We want someone to tell us what to do, like a doctor, and then write a prescription that will cure our problem. We want someone to wave a magic wand and make it all better. But we don't want to have to do anything. After all, aren't our lives already too busy with the kids, our jobs, cleaning house, paying bills, repairing our cars? Adding another piece of work would just be too much.

I often hear that my clients have not done their homework because they were too busy. I start to wonder about their investment in each other. Questions come to mind, like:

Why are they too busy to spend the time on their marriage?
Why does it seem like other things are more important?
Why are they even coming to counseling?
Why do they just want to complain about their problems, point fingers at each other and spend time in my office?

I often confront this issue and explain the process further, emphasizing the importance of following the recommended homework assignments. I further explain that this is not a temporary course of action, but the success of counseling is dependent on the work they do now. It will affect the rest of their life together. Many times, this changes the way they have been viewing the counseling, and compliance with the process gets better. Other times, some clients decide counseling is not the way they need to go.

For this gift of a lifetime to be ongoing, it has to be practiced daily. With commitment, dedication, and patience, and by keeping the "FACTS and FAITH" in your daily life, you can be the creator of a marriage that lasts a lifetime. Reading and applying this book with your spouse could be the first step in creating a marriage that *is both joyous and fulfilling.* Please use the following pages to turn your reading of this book into activities and strategies that extend your love affair with your spouse.

Appendix A

I hope after reading this book:

You are able to make strong decisions and are willing to follow through with them;

You try to understand your partner's needs, and feel that your partner's needs are on a level with your own;

You get in touch with your own feelings, and share them with your spouse;

You practice the FACTS every day;

You appreciate the elements of FAITH;

Your communication is flowing and information is being received without ambiguity;

Your marriage is top priority, and its survival your top commitment.

Place this book on the coffee table, leave it in the sunroom, or leave it by the bed. Just seeing it there will remind you of your commitment and what is required to preserve it.

Use the Maintenance Agreement and suggestions at the end of the book as reminders of your commitment to each other.

Share this book with your spouse; give it as a gift to others and refer back to it often.

Give this book to your children as a wedding gift. They can give copies to their friends.

It is important to know that marriage is worth working on, that family is important, and that people need help in preserving their relationships.

We have many documents in our lives that require renewals. We renew our driver's licenses every few years; we renew our professional licenses; and we renew our credit cards when they expire.

Why isn't marriage included in the renewal process? It can be included, and you can make it happen. Every year on your anniversary date, you can renew your vows. That is your choice and can be part of your lifetime plan. What if yearly renewals were mandatory for all marriages? People would probably be more attentive during the year and plan better. Maybe people would cherish their marriages more because of the yearly proclamation of their love.

Appendix B

Creating New Vows

Now it is up to you to write the vows you want to use each year on your anniversary. That is the last part of *The Gift of a Lifetime* and the beginning of your forever.

Write your own vows on the accompanying page. Make them a fresh and reinvigorated way of annually celebrating the gift you both continue to give to each other.

Wedding Vows

_____

_____

_____

_____

_____

_____

_____

_____

_____

_____

_____

_____

_____

_____

_____

_____

_____

Wedding Vows

_____

_____

_____

_____

_____

_____

_____

_____

_____

_____

_____

_____

_____

_____

_____

_____

Appendix C

Maintenance Agreement

As I tell all of my clients on the very first meeting: I give homework. The reason for that is to encourage them to keep their relationship the number one priority in their daily lives at all times.

Reading this book is the first step in building a marriage that lasts a lifetime. The next step will need to be taken by you. You can think of it as your insurance policy or a spoken promise. I call it a "Maintenance Agreement," and it sounds like this:

> *I agree to keep my marriage as my utmost priority and work on it every day. I will not allow any cause be a reason to forget my agreement. It is my hope that my everlasting love for you and this agreement will help me achieve the gift of a lifetime. The FACTS and the FAITH will be my guide.*

The following pages contain some thoughtful ways to help you live up to the agreement. Keeping love alive in a marriage is hard work, but the rewards are great.

My wish is that these suggestions will enrich your marriage and transform it into a more loving and accepting marriage that can stand the test of time. Be creative and personalize the following to fit your unique situation.

Above all, as Larry James writes, "Celebrate Love, and say 'I love you' at least once every day."

Thinking: Journaling about the FACTS

Keep a daily journal of your reflections on FACTS and how you can practice them. Here are some suggestions:

- What things do you still need to FORGIVE? This includes past hurts and present resentments. Only by focusing on why you have those feelings can you work toward releasing them.

- Write all the things you ACCEPT about your spouse on a daily basis. Note them in positive language. Be careful to avoid mention of making sacrifices for your acceptance.

- Record the COMPASSIONATE actions you see your spouse initiate, whether they are toward you or for others. Reflect on his or her attitude as evidenced by these actions.

- Journal about any difficulties you have with TRUST in your relationship. Where do you feel trust weakening? What specific conditions make you prone to lose trust in your spouse?

- Build a SPIRITUAL dialogue into your journal, in which you try to capture feelings that you have about your purpose, gifts, or sensitivities. Write a letter to your spouse addressing the moments between you that are the most spiritual.

Find a time and place to share these with your spouse. Invite him or her to respond to moments in the journal that you view differently. Encourage your spouse to see your journaling reflections as the evidence of the importance of the relationship to you.

Acting: Practicing the FACTS

Forgiveness

Teach forgiveness to your children, and let them see it at work.

Acceptance

Be kind to yourself and learn how to love who you are.

Teach acceptance to your children, and let them observe it as you and your spouse practice unconditional love.

Compassion

Like the bumper sticker says, practice random acts of kindness. Challenge yourself to improve one person's day to work out your compassionate "muscles."

Trust

Always be honest with your spouse. Above all, be honest with yourself. Say what you mean and mean what you say.

Trust is built every day. It is one of the cornerstones of the marriage commitment and referred to as a promise. Remind yourself of the vow you took and make the words live on. Be repetitious in actions that are trustworthy.

Spirituality

Share your spiritual journey with each other.

Worship and pray according to your beliefs.

This book was written with love, compassion, and dedication to preserve the institution of marriage the way God intended.

I leave you with this quote by Andrea Maurois:
"Marriage is an edifice that must be rebuilt every day."

Let this be the first day in the rebuilding of yours.

Sincerely,

Barbara

The Serenity Prayer

God grant me the serenity
to accept the things I cannot change;
courage to change the things I can;
and wisdom to know the difference.

-Reinhold Niebuhr

Bibliography

Bucket List, The. Dir. Rob Reiner. Warner Brothers, 2008.

Coombs, Robert. "Marital Status and Personal Well-Being: A Literature Review." *Family Relations* 40 (1991): 97-102.

Dailey, Jim. "Preparing for Eternity – On Purpose: A Conversation with Rick Warren." *Decision.* Billy Graham Evangelistic Association. Nov. 2004. Web. 16 Oct. 2009.

Dayton, Tian, *The Magic of Forgiveness.* Deerfield Beach, Florida: Health Communications, Inc., 2003.

Dobson, James. *Love for a Lifetime.* Sisters, Oregon: Multnomah Books, 1993.

Fine, Arnold. "Letter in a Wallet." *Reader's Digest*, Sept. 1985. Originally published by the Jewish Press, New York, in 1984.

Fireproof. Dir. Alex Kendrick. Samuel Goldwyn Films, 2008. Film.

Frankel, Victor E. *Man's Search for Meaning.* New York: Washington Square Press, 1984.

Fromm, Eric. *The Art of Loving.* New York: Harper, 1956.

Gibran, Kahlil. *The Prophet.* New York: Alfred A. Knopf, Inc., 1923.

Gottman, John M., and Nan Silver. *The Seven Principles for Making Marriage Work.* New York: Orion mass market paperback, 2004. Print.

Gray, John. *Men Are from Mars, Women Are from Venus: The Classic Guide to Understanding the Opposite Sex.* New York: Harper Paperbacks, 2004.

Gurman, Alan S., and Neil S. Jacobsen (eds). *Clinical Handbook of Couple Therapy*, 3rd ed. New York: Guilford Press, 2002.

James, Larry. *How to Really Love the One You're With*. Scottsdale, Arizona: Career Assurance Press, 1994.

Kendrick, Stephen and Alex Kendrick. *The Love Dare*. Nashville, Tennessee: B&H Publishing, 2008.

McCormick, James R. *Marriage Is For Adults*. Self-published, 2007.

Lewis, Jordana and Jerry Adler. "Forgive and Let Live." *Newsweek*. 27 Sept. 2004.

Love, Patricia. *The Truth About Love-The Highs, the Lows, and How You Can Make It Last Forever*. New York: Fireside, 2001.

Oliviero, Helen. "Caring for aging parents tough, rewarding." *Atlanta Journal Constitution*. 22 Mar. 2009.

Olsen, David. *The Spiritual Work of Marriage*. New York: Routledge, 2008.

Osteen, Joel. *Your Best Life Now: 7 Steps to Living at Your Full Potential*. New York: Warner Faith, 2004.

Peck, M. Scott. *The Road Less Traveled*. New York: Simon & Schuster, 1978.

Prather, Hugh. *The Little Book of Letting Go*. Conari Press, California, 2000.

Schwartz, Richard C. *You Are the One You've Been Waiting For*. Oak Park, Illinois: Trailheads, 2008.

Stack, S. and J.R. Eshleman. "Marital status and happiness: A 17-nation study." *Journal of Marriage and the Family*. 60:2 (1998) 527-536.

Thomas, A. "Andrea and Cliff Riley help blended families unite." *Business Innovators Magazine* (2019) online: https://businessinnovatorsmagazine. com/andrea-and-cliff-riley-help-blended-families-unite/

Waite, Linda and Maggie Gallagher. *The Case for Marriage: Why Married People Are Happier, Healthier, and Better off Financially.* New York: Broadway Books, 2000.

Waller, Robert James. *The Bridges of Madison County.* New York: Warner Books, 1992.

ABOUT BARBARA

Phil Winter Photography

I grew up in Long Island, New York. My early years were mostly uneventful until I realized that my family had some relationship problems. My mother and father separated when I was only 4 and got back together when I was 12. In my later years, as I witnessed many friends and family struggle in their relationships I began to want to help others. My own relationships were struggling too. I was focused on finding an answer and realized it is not who you find, but who you are.

I wear many hats. I am a Registered Nurse, Licensed Professional Counselor, Coach, and author. I am passionate about helping people improve their relationships. Whether in a counseling setting or through individual coaching I am dedicated to each and every client, no matter what they bring to the table. We work as a team to make the life changes they need.

I earned a Bachelor of Arts in Sociology from C.W. Post College of Long Island University, a Bachelor of Sciences in Nursing from Stony Brook University, and a Master of Science in Counseling from Georgia State University. I am also certified by the National Board of Certified Counselors.

I continue to write relationship blog posts and am working on a new book—all focusing on helping people make positive changes. With my books, using many of my own life challenges as a wife and mother in addition to my experience counseling couples, I am able to take my reader on the road to a lasting marriage. The tools I suggest are realistic, usable, and have proven successful for many. My hope is that my readers will walk away with useful information, skills, and ideas that are easy to incorporate in their relationships.

Please visit me at www.barbarajpeters.com.

Printed in the United States
By Bookmasters